CW01507014

Paul Ricoeur and Environmental Philosophy

STUDIES IN THE THOUGHT OF PAUL RICOEUR

Series Editors
Greg S. Johnson, University of Providence;
and Dan R. Stiver, Hardin-Simmons University

Studies in the Thought of Paul Ricoeur, a series in conjunction with the Society for Ricoeur Studies, aims to generate research on Ricoeur, about whom interest is rapidly growing both nationally (United States and Canada) and internationally. Broadly construed, the series has three interrelated themes. First, we develop the historical connections to and in Ricoeur's thought. Second, we extend Ricoeur's dialogue with contemporary thinkers representing a variety of disciplines. Third, we utilize Ricoeur to address future prospects in philosophy and other fields that respond to emerging issues of importance. The series approaches these themes from the belief that Ricoeur's thought is not just suited to theoretical exchanges, but can and does matter for how we actually engage in the many dimensions that constitute lived existence.

Recent Titles in the Series

Paul Ricoeur and Environmental Philosophy

David Utsler

LEXINGTON BOOKS
Lanham • Boulder • New York • London

Published by Lexington Books
An imprint of The Rowman & Littlefield Publishing Group, Inc.
4501 Forbes Boulevard, Suite 200, Lanham, Maryland 20706
www.rowman.com

86-90 Paul Street, London EC2A 4NE

Copyright © 2024 by The Rowman & Littlefield Publishing Group, Inc.

All rights reserved. No part of this book may be reproduced in any form or by any electronic or mechanical means, including information storage and retrieval systems, without
written permission from the publisher, except by a reviewer who may quote passages
in a review.

British Library Cataloguing in Publication Information Available

Library of Congress Cataloging-in-Publication Data

Names: Utsler, David, author.
Title: Paul Ricoeur and environmental philosophy / David Utsler.
Description: Lanham : Lexington Books, [2024] | Series: Studies in the
  thought of Paul Ricoeur | Includes bibliographical references and index.
Identifiers: LCCN 2024024887 (print) | LCCN 2024024888 (ebook) | ISBN
  9781666924893 (cloth) | ISBN 9781666924909 (ebook)
Subjects: LCSH: Ricœur, Paul. | Environmental sciences--Philosophy.
Classification: LCC B2430.R554 U87 2024 (print) | LCC B2430.R554 (ebook)
  | DDC 304.201--dc23/eng/20240627
LC record available at https://lccn.loc.gov/2024024887
LC ebook record available at https://lccn.loc.gov/2024024888

For Mena, Brendan, and Sophie

Contents

Preface

From Hermeneutics to Environmental Hermeneutics

Paul Ricoeur and Environmental Philosophy is a return to an original inspiration. My introduction to philosophical hermeneutics came during my undergraduate studies when I took a course titled "Husserl and His Commentators." One of the course readings was Ricoeur's essay "Phenomenology and Hermeneutics."[1] From that reading, I became deeply interested in reading much more of Ricoeur and the study of philosophical hermeneutics more generally. For me, hermeneutics became a default organizing principle for thought and for being. Conservatively, my claim is not that hermeneutics says everything about everything that needs to be or could be said. I do not wish to fall into the trap of thinking that this particular philosophical approach is the ultimate end to what the entire history of philosophy was leading just because it is something that was illuminating for me (yes, many philosophers are not without guilt here). Still, hermeneutics does touch the fundamental condition of human experience—our necessarily inescapable drive to *understand* and make sense of the world about us. Life is an insatiable quest for meaning, even in the smallest quotidian things.[2] And I would further say (perhaps less conservatively) that, as such, hermeneutics represents the fundamental gesture of philosophy.[3] To wonder, to examine ourselves and others, as Socrates said lovers of wisdom ought to do, is to engage in interpretation.

Not surprisingly, the same professor and mentor who introduced me to the work of Paul Ricoeur also introduced me to environmental philosophy over twenty years ago. I attended the annual conference of the International Association for Environmental Philosophy (IAEP) where he was presenting a paper. Most of his work in environmental philosophy revolved around Max Scheler and Maurice Merleau-Ponty rather than Ricoeur, but I did hear a presentation in that conference employing Gadamer in environmental philosophy. I continued attending the IAEP each year but had not submitted a paper of my own the first few years. I finally decided I had something I wanted to contribute.

I had been working through Ricoeur's *Oneself as Another*[4] when it occurred to me that his "hermeneutics of the self" had possibilities for rich applications to environmental philosophy. For my paper, I focused on a single concept for which I used the term "environmental identity," although not so originally as I had supposed. Robert Melchior Figueroa had coined the term in his work on environmental justice some years previously, and "environmental identity" had also just begun to be used in the field of environmental psychology.[5] My work was the first to develop the concept of environmental identity from a hermeneutic perspective and, at that time, a particularly Ricoeurian one.

The following year I presented a paper at the Society for Ricoeur Studies, which was published a year later in *Philosophy Today* as "Paul Ricoeur's Hermeneutics as a Model for Environmental Philosophy."[6] Since that time I have continued to publish about, among other things, hermeneutics and environmental philosophy, and many of my conference presentations over the years have been in that area. Back at that IAEP conference where I first presented a paper on Ricoeur and environmental philosophy, I also met Brian Treanor of Loyola Marymount University and Forrest Clingerman of Ohio Northern University. One year later, at a conference hosted by the Working Group for Religion, Ethics, and Nature at Ohio Northern, I also met Martin Drenthen. A collaboration between the four of us ensued that eventually led to the publication of the first book dedicated to "environmental hermeneutics" as a distinct field of environmental philosophy titled *Interpreting Nature: The Emerging Field of Environmental Hermeneutics.*[7]

DETOUR AND RETURN

Environmental hermeneutics continues to grow into an ever-widening field representing many hermeneutical approaches to environmental philosophy as well as environmental justice concerns. At the time I am writing this, a follow-up volume to *Interpreting Nature* is in the works with several contributors from varied backgrounds wherein we intend to demonstrate the expanding scope of environmental hermeneutics and its broad application. Hermeneutics clarifies the conditions of understanding and is by no means reducible to fanciful thoughts about the environment. Quite to the contrary, hermeneutics has the tools to address itself directly to concrete environmental challenges in our day.

This book, however, returns to my original endeavors into the discourse of hermeneutics and environmental philosophy, which is to explore the ways in which Paul Ricoeur's hermeneutics serve as a model to address environmental concerns. What I propose in this text is a specifically Ricoeurian environmental hermeneutics. I also take this book to be merely an introduction to such, as I am not claiming to present a complete or exhaustive environmental hermeneutics constructed from Ricoeur's thought. I am certain that the contents of this book only begin to uncover the potentialities in Ricoeur's corpus that can realize a comprehensive Ricoeurian environmental hermeneutics.

Since those first investigations into the hermeneutics of Paul Ricoeur and environmental philosophy, I have taken numerous detours into many other aspects of environmental hermeneutics. *Paul Ricoeur and Environmental Philosophy* represents a return to that original project.

NOTES

1. Paul Ricoeur, "Phenomenology and Hermeneutics," in *Hermeneutics and the Human Sciences: Essays on Language, Action, and Interpretation*, edited and translated by John B. Thompson (Cambridge, UK: Cambridge University Press, 1981), 101–28. This essay is also in Ricoeur's *From Text to Action: Essays in Hermeneutics, II*, translated by Kathleen Blamey and John B. Thompson (Evanston, IL: Northwestern University Press, 1991), 25–52.

2. Richard Palmer insightfully observes: "In fact, from the time you wake in the morning until you sink into sleep, you are 'interpreting.' On waking you glance at the bedside clock and interpret its meaning: you recall what day it is, and in grasping the meaning of the day you are already primordially recalling to yourself the way you are placed in the world and your plans for the future; you rise and must interpret the words and gestures of those you meet on the daily round. Interpretation is, then, perhaps the most basic act of human thinking; indeed, existing itself may be said to be a constant process of interpretation." *Hermeneutics: Interpretation Theory in Schleiermacher, Dilthey, Heidegger, and Gadamer* (Evanston, IL: Northwestern University Press, 1969), 8–9.

3. Cf. James Risser, *The Life of Understanding: A Contemporary Hermeneutics* (Bloomington: Indiana University Press, 2012).

4. Paul Ricoeur, *Oneself as Another*, translated by Kathleen Blamey (Chicago: University of Chicago Press, 1992).

5. See Susan Clayton and Susan Opotow, editors, *Identity and the Natural Environment: The Psychological Significance of Nature* (Cambridge, MA: MIT Press, 2003).

6. David Utsler, "Paul Ricoeur's Hermeneutics as a Model for Environmental Philosophy" in *Philosophy Today* 53, no. 2 (Summer 2009): 173–78.

7. Forrest Clingerman, Brian Treanor, Martin Drenthen, and David Utsler, editors, *Interpreting Nature: The Emerging Field of Environmental Hermeneutics* (New York: Fordham University Press, 2014).

Acknowledgments

I first wish to acknowledge the staff at Lexington Books whose hard work and expertise brought the final product of this book together. I particularly want to thank Jana Hodges-Kluck, Deanna Biondi, and Samuel Withers who worked with me throughout the publication process and whose constant encouragement, patience, and guidance were invaluable. I am equally grateful to Greg S. Johnson and Dan R. Stiver, editors of the series Studies in the Thought of Paul Ricoeur, for all their work in this series and for believing that this book makes a worthy contribution to it. In this same vein, I wish to express my gratitude to the Society for Ricoeur Studies (SRS) that, in conjunction with Lexington Press, created this series. My many years of being a part of this society and the privilege of presenting my research at the annual conference allowed me to reflect more deeply about my work and to bring greater clarity to it. There are aspects in this present work that were presented early on at the SRS, and which were no doubt greatly improved as a result of the gracious feedback and critique SRS members provided. Here I must mention David Pellauer, who, as president of the SRS at that time, encouraged the publication of one of my very first papers that explored the intersection of the thought of Paul Ricoeur and environmental philosophy. David also made me aware of Ricoeur's only substantial commentary on ecological issues, which became the primary subject matter of the first chapter.

I owe a great debt of gratitude to my friends and colleagues Nathan M. Bell, Christina M. Gschwandtner, and Brian Treanor, who looked at early drafts of some of the chapters. They provided indispensable feedback that made those chapters much more readable than they would have been otherwise and forced me to think through my arguments more clearly. More importantly, I am especially grateful for the years of friendship and conversation that we have shared on Paul Ricoeur, philosophical hermeneutics, and environmental philosophy, among other topics. Philosophy is best done in dialogue with others. Nathan, Christina, and Brian have been among the very best of those "others" for me. Such friendships make for becoming a better philosopher.

As this is my first book of which I am the sole author, I would deem it inconsiderate not to mention John R. White and David M. Kaplan. John because, as my undergraduate mentor, he first introduced me to Paul Ricoeur and the importance of hermeneutics. David because, as my graduate advisor, he continued to build on that foundation and cultivate my admiration of Paul Ricoeur's philosophy and of hermeneutics generally. The good fortune I had to have them as professors provided me with the foundation that evolved into much of my professional work. As has been said many, many times of such influences, any lack or shortcoming in my work is certainly mine alone. John and David, however, do share in the credit for whatever worthwhile contributions this book makes to the ongoing philosophical conversation.

Introduction

A Ricoeurian Environmental Hermeneutics

Paul Ricoeur was a prolific writer, producing a vast body of work throughout his career, engaging a wide variety of thinkers and philosophical movements. While there are certain landmark works in his philosophical trajectory, there is not a single book one could isolate as *the* seminal work in his corpus as the sun around which his subsequent work orbited. There are recurring themes and inquiries that thread their way throughout his intellectual tapestry but no single, defining magnum opus. Amid his vast corpus, however, one does not find Ricoeur addressing environmental crises or proposing a hermeneutics or phenomenology of the environment. The only published article of which I am aware in which Ricoeur spoke of the environment and the ecological crisis at any length is a 1993 interview, recently translated into English as "Ethics, Politics, Ecology.[1]

The title *Paul Ricoeur and Environmental Philosophy* does not suggest, therefore, that this book is about any detailed or extensive philosophical reflection that Ricoeur ever did about environmental issues or an examination or analysis of his environmental hermeneutics. Simply put, Paul Ricoeur was not an environmental philosopher. While it would be difficult to avoid altogether simply "making connections" or "applying" Ricoeur's hermeneutics to environmental thought, this book represents more than that. The underlying motivation to write this book is the insistence that Ricoeur's philosophical hermeneutics is relevant to elucidating ways of being-in-the-world germane to the relationship with the other-than-human world in which we dwell. Hermeneutics deeply involves the idea that life is a continual process of understanding—understanding the world about us and, in that process, understanding ourselves in relation to it. Understanding, in turn, motivates and guides action and ethics.[2] Thus, I propose that hermeneutics has a great deal to offer environmental thought in general and environmental philosophy in particular.

1

ENVIRONMENTAL PHILOSOPHY: YESTERDAY
AND TODAY

For readers unfamiliar with environmental philosophy, I provide here just a cursory overview of its prehistory and history. At roughly a half century, environmental philosophy is still a young subdiscipline of philosophy. The environmental movement is generally understood to have been inspired by Rachel Carson's *Silent Spring*,[3] a book which caused such public outrage that it led to the ban of the pesticide DDT. *Silent Spring* raised the collective consciousness of the dangers the postwar world, especially with the chemical industry, posed to the environment and to human life. Within eight years after the publication of *Silent Spring*, Richard Nixon created the Environmental Protection Agency, its first administrator, William Ruckelshaus, being sworn in on December 4, 1970.[4] The first Earth Day had been observed that same year on April 22.

With a concern for what the relationship ought to be between humans and the natural world, it is no surprise that philosophers began asking questions. Environmental philosophy, more broadly, grew out of what was originally a philosophical focus on ethical issues related to the environment. And why not? After all, as Eugene Hargrove observed, philosophy was the wellspring from which "most academic and scientific disciplines" emerged, and that up until the middle of the nineteenth century, "scientists were still called, and thought of themselves, as natural philosophers."[5] It certainly seemed appropriate for philosophy to return to thinking about the natural world, especially as a response to the growing awareness of an environmental crisis. While the "hard sciences" are, quite obviously, necessary to address the environmental crisis, the physical sciences alone are not adequate. The role of philosophy is to examine assumptions as to what we think about, why we think about this and not that, how we think, and, most importantly, how what we think shapes what we do. The answer to the environmental crisis cannot be in science alone—after all, it is underlying philosophical assumptions that led to uses of science and technology that are largely to blame for the crisis. Solutions to the challenges we face must be truly interdisciplinary and cooperative.

In addition to Eugene Hargrove, some other early figures in the founding of environmental ethics include J. Baird Callicott, Holmes Rolston III, Richard Routley, Arne Ness, and Max Oelschlaeger, among others. Professional societies and associations were later formed such as the International Society for Environmental Ethics (ISEE) and the International Association for Environmental Philosophy (IAEP), along with their journals *Environmental Ethics* and *Environmental Philosophy*, respectively. Many such scholarly organizations in multiple disciplines have arisen. Many central issues in environmental ethics included the problems with anthropocentrism, whether other beings in nature have intrinsic or only instrumental value, what are our responsibilities to the natural world and to future generations, and the rights of animals. Today, environmental philosophy is very broad to include things like environmental aesthetics, ecophenomenology, ecofeminism, and, of course, more recently, environmental hermeneutics.

ENVIRONMENTAL HERMENEUTICS

Environmental hermeneutics stems from the conviction that as human beings, interpretation is basic to lived experience. Hermeneutics recognizes our fundamental drive to find meaning in life. Hermeneutics also recognizes that none of us think or act from nowhere. We are, essentially, finite beings situated at particular times in history, and such placement creates the conditions for understanding. Environmental philosophy, generally, might consider a metaphysics of nature or reflect upon what nature means aesthetically, but hermeneutics is practiced substantially more "on the ground," as it were. There is never a pure and unmediated experience of the environment. We interpret environments and those interpretations take place within the hermeneutic circle that consists of language, culture, and pre-understandings, known or unknown, that we have. Some see nature as only "resource," while other peoples will refer to nature as home or kin. These are all interpretations.

For readers who are perhaps unfamiliar with philosophical hermeneutics, interpretation does not mean mere opinion or pure subjective reflection. Hermeneutics recognizes that meaning is not a matter of a subject who encounters an object, who then deciphers some singular, fixed meaning the object has. Rather, the encounter between a subject and the world about her or him is always a mediated encounter in which meaning comes out of the "event" of that encounter. Hermeneutics is a dialectic between what we already know (the familiar) and what we do not yet understand (the alien), as we seek to expand our horizon of understanding. In his editor's introduction to Gadamer's *Philosophical Hermeneutics*, David E. Linge writes that "the hermeneutical has to do with bridging the gap between the familiar world in which we stand and the strange meaning that resists assimilation into the horizons of our world."[6]

Lastly, hermeneutics is acutely aware of the role of language in shaping our perception and understanding of the world. This is of utmost importance for environmental hermeneutics. Understanding the world is not a matter of apprehending pure facts. Quite the contrary, facts can be and are understood in a myriad of ways and the meaning of facts are not always apparent. Where meaning is not apparent, philosophical hermeneutics begins. Environmental hermeneutics exists because we are in a species-threatening environmental crisis that calls for interpretation. The future of humanity and that of the environment will result from interpretation. So, it is not a question of interpretation or no interpretation, but how self-consciously we will interpret, and whether those interpretations will guide us to a healthy future or to extinction.

TOWARD A RICOEURIAN
ENVIRONMENTAL HERMENEUTICS

The hermeneutical tradition is broad and has many tributaries. The joining of hermeneutics and environmental thought can be explored down an extensive variety of avenues. For this book series Studies in the Thought of Paul Ricoeur, this current work will focus on cultivating an environmental hermeneutics from the soil of the thought of Ricoeur, specifically. I have probably spent as much time thinking about aspects of Ricoeur's work that I am leaving out as I have those that I have included. And I am certain there is much of Ricoeur's philosophy that I have not yet thought of that would be important for a hermeneutics of the environment. Truly, the purpose of this book is to simply "introduce" Ricoeur's hermeneutics to environmental thought.

There are six chapters to this book. Chapter 1 looks at the interview I referred to at the start of this introduction. Despite the fact that this interview was conducted three decades ago and that Ricoeur was not an environmental philosopher, the interview, nonetheless, shows Ricoeur's grasp of some key issues as we face the ecological crisis. I will cover Ricoeur's perspective on technoscience, the will to survive and the ethics of responsibility, our responsibility to the future, how Ricoeur mediated human difference along with being a part of the ecosystem, and his thoughts on the integration of ecology with justice in politics. Although not formally philosophical, this interview contains tremendous insight and wisdom for addressing today's environmental challenges in what has been called a new geological epoch, the Anthropocene.

Chapter 2 will build upon the concept of environmental identity. In environmental hermeneutics, Ricoeur's "hermeneutics of the self" has been drawn upon to consider our concept of self in relation to environments. Each of us has an environmental identity and we also share in collective environmental identities. The specific focus of this chapter is on the corporeality of environmental identity. That is, how environmental identity is embodied. The environment that forms our environmental identity is not abstract. Rather, it is material. Our encounter with environments takes place in the flesh. How we interact with and encounter our physical environment in our bodies is crucial to how our environmental identity is constituted. Our disembodied electronic world of social media and Zoom, despite the benefits they bring, actually pose a threat to environmental identity to a great extent. For so many of us in contemporary society, an embodied dwelling in the so-called natural world has become alien.

Chapter 3 looks at the continuing debate in environmental philosophy over anthropocentrism and the many forms of non-anthropocentrism that are argued should supplant it. I look at the basics in how anthropocentrism and non-anthropocentrism are conceived and argue for a hermeneutic alternative. Ultimately, the binary either/or approach to these questions I take to be lacking and insufficient to address the human relationship to the natural world. Based on Ricoeur's hermeneutics, I will argue for what can be called "polycentrism" or "multicentrism," and that the complexities of the environment call for a more dialectical approach that recognizes the legitimate claims of many "centers" of moral concern.

Chapter 4 considers fragility, both the fragility of the earth and, even more so, the fragility of the human species. Ricoeur observed during the 1993 interview, "Ethics, Politics, Ecology," that for humanity to survive, nature must survive. We have a great dependence on the earth for our survival, but if we fail to survive, the earth will do just fine. I cite environmental philosopher Keith R. Peterson on the asymmetric dependence we have on the earth. Human fragility demands that we take responsibility for the environmental crisis. We live in the midst of the sixth mass extinction and an alarming rate of the loss of biodiversity, much of which has been caused by human activity. If we fail to take responsibility, our fragility will guarantee our own eventual extinction.

Chapter 5, then, takes up the question of responsibility, what I call in this chapter a poetics of responsibility. The nature of the environmental crisis is such that we must be forward-looking in our quest for solutions, hence a "poetics." I look at Ricoeur's hermeneutics of imagination and initiative as the means to enact this poetics of environmental responsibility. I offer a brief interlude to discuss the relationship of responsibility to the field of environmental justice before returning to the topics of narrative and the promise as important components in responsibility.

The final chapter, chapter 6, is directed to the question of whether Ricoeur's text-centered hermeneutics can be useful for environmental hermeneutics. The basis of this question focuses on the idea of the "metaphor of the text" or the "book of nature." My belief is that nature or the environment (or any object of interpretation that is not a text) need not be looked upon as a text in order to engage in interpretive activity. Despite the long history of text interpretation in hermeneutics, interpretation *as such*, is more general than the interpretation of texts. Interpreting is a fundamental human activity in which we engage constantly in everything. If this more general theory of interpretation is the case, then it raises the question if Ricoeur's hermeneutics, being mostly centered on the interpretation of texts, is workable for a more general environmental hermeneutics. I argue that Ricoeur's text-centered hermeneutics can be understood as a subset of a more general hermeneutics that offers many tools for environmental hermeneutics.

It is my intention and hope that this book will be useful both to those who work in Ricoeur studies and well as environmental philosophers who are open to new philosophical perspectives to address current environmental challenges. It is also my hope that *Paul Ricoeur and Environmental Philosophy* will encourage more interest in the potential for his work to address environmental issues effectively.[7] Finally, I hope that this book enlarges and contributes to discourse for environmental hermeneutics generally, helping the field continue to expand.

NOTES

1. "L'éthique, le politique, l'écologie. Entretien avec Paul Ricoeur" [Propos recueillis par Edith et Jean Paul Deléage]. *Ecologie Politique. Sciences, Culture, Société*, 1993, n°7, été. My gratitude to David Pellauer for making me aware of this interview some years ago. The recent English translation "Ethics, Politics, Ecology" can be found in Paul Ricoeur, *Philosophy, Ethics, & Politics*, translated by Kathleen Blamey (Cambridge, UK: Polity Press, 2020), 103–16.

2. For a recent and excellent contribution to the relationship of hermeneutics to ethics from a primarily Gadamerian perspective, see Theodore George, *The Responsibility to Understand: Hermeneutical Contours of the Ethical Life* (Edinburgh: Edinburgh University Press, 2020).

3. Rachel Carson, *Silent Spring*, 50th Anniversary Edition (Boston: Mariner Books, 2002). *Silent Spring* was originally published in 1962.

4. See https://www.epa.gov/history/origins-epa.

5. Eugene C. Hargrove, *Foundations of Environmental Ethics* (Denton: Environmental Ethics Books, 1989), 43.

6. David E. Linge, "Editor's Introduction," in Hans-Georg Gadamer, *Philosophical Hermeneutics*, translated and edited by David E. Linge (Berkeley: University of California Press, 1976), xii.

7. To a great extent, this has already begun. See *Interpreting Nature: The Emerging Field of Environmental Hermeneutics*, edited by Forrest Clingerman, Brian Treanor, Martin Drenthen, and David Utsler (New York: Fordham University Press, 2014).

Chapter 1

Paul Ricoeur on the Ecological Crisis

Paul Ricoeur, as noted in the introduction, was not an environmental philosopher and never directly addressed any aspect of environmental problems in any formal philosophical study. He did, however, as also noted in the introduction, speak concerning the ecological crisis in a 1993 interview titled "Ethics, Politics, Ecology."[1] While not a formal philosophical analysis, his comments raise insightful points that remain relevant to the current discourse in environmental philosophy. In subsequent chapters, I will return to some of these points in more depth, specifically in relation to discussions in contemporary environmental philosophy and ethics.

Ricoeur discussed the ecological crisis under the rubric of responsibility (a theme that I will take up more fully in chapter 5, "A Poetics of Environmental Responsibility"). Some of the key points in the interview are as follows. The scope of our responsibility in addressing the ecological crisis is in direct proportion to the scale of the crisis, which is global. This scale requires international institutions to address the problems although, Ricoeur laments, no such institutions exist. Our responsibility and our response must be forward looking—an idea that Ricoeur takes from Hans Jonas and his ethics of responsibility. Specifically, beyond looking at immediate and present consequences, the threat to our survival necessitates the consideration of the potential long-term, not yet realized, consequences of our actions. Further, we must properly balance human difference from other nonhuman entities with our being a fragment of the ecosystem (or what many simply refer to as being a part of nature) as we undertake our responsibility. Finally, Ricoeur suggests that issues of social justice are also linked to ecological problems (while Ricoeur does not use the term, his comments fall into the area of environmental justice—i.e., issues of social justice within an environmental context).[2] Given that the vast scale of harm to the planet by human activity is the result of discoveries and advances in science and technology, it seems appropriate to discuss Ricoeur's comments on technoscience to set up the larger context of his overall comments. Thus, I begin there.

SCIENCE, TECHNOLOGY, AND THE
AGE OF TECHNOSCIENCE

When asked about the term "technoscience," Ricoeur replied, "The very fact that it is a composite term should remind us that its components are, at certain stages of knowledge, independent, and others merge together."[3] This distinction is important to Ricoeur. He places science under the umbrella of knowledge sought solely because of the human desire to know—i.e., knowledge for its own sake, not for any benefit we might gain from it. To refer to Aristotle, as human beings we begin by "wondering that things are as they are" (*Metaphysics*, Bk. 1, Ch. 2, 983a, 15), not what we can do with them or how we can benefit from them. Technology, by contrast, Ricoeur defines as the application of scientific discoveries to various purposes and ends on our part. This is a simple distinction between what knowledge *is* and how knowledge is *used*. The scientist, therefore, is not to be held to account for the ways in which technology harnesses a discovery. Ricoeur gives the example that Einstein's work may have made space travel possible, but he cannot be held responsible that nuclear devices are placed in orbit.[4]

If science is knowledge (*scientia*) about how nature works gathered from observing its processes, technology is the use of that knowledge for human ends. It can be said that technology makes greater scientific discovery possible (e.g., the telescope). If science is about observing—i.e., "seeing"—technology has produced instruments that aid human ability to observe, a point Don Ihde has made.[5] Ricoeur's distinction, however, remains valid. Science precedes technology insofar as technological instruments and practices are built on knowledge gained from scientific observation. In cases where technology precedes greater scientific advancement by providing instrumentation that aids in scientific observation, science remains knowledge for its own sake, driven only by the desire to know, and technology is the employment of scientific knowledge for some purpose beyond itself. So, with Ricoeur, we are mindful that a composite term indicates the independence of each part prior to their merging together. How shall this merging, then, be understood? What is "technoscience"? Technoscience, in Ricoeur's words, is the "technological extension of science."[6] How is the term "technoscience" any different from simple technology, especially if technology is an application of scientific discovery? Is that not merely an "extension"? At first glance, it seems that "technology" and "technoscience" each essentially refer to the same thing. Yes, technology is taking knowledge from scientific discovery, using it to achieve desired ends. This is true for the invention of anything from the hammer to rocket ships. Technology is the application of scientific knowledge to solve problems, create more convenience and ease of life, or even for recreation and entertainment. Technoscience, even more than mere application, is the appropriation of science, not as knowledge as an end in itself, but at the service of the ends of technology.

The grammar of the term is revealing. "Technoscience" is a compressed term (a merger of two terms as Ricoeur said) of what would be the longer "technology-science." For example, if I would refer to "health-science," you immediately know that I am referring to scientific research that has human health and physical well-being as its end. In its mere grammatical sense, technoscience is neither good nor bad; it simply refers to scientific research that is carried out specifically to create technological means to serve various ends. Many of these ends are perceived and welcomed as very good. The issue and danger with technology-science, however, is the capacity for unforeseen or unintended ends, the consequences of which are dire and cannot be controlled. One line of thinking is that technoscience itself can provide the remedy for whatever unforeseen and unintended negative effects it might cause. But what guarantee can technoscience offer that even its fixes will not also have unforeseen deleterious effects?

Ihde's explanation of technoscience is helpful here. He writes: "Technoscience is the hybrid output of science and technology, now bound inextricably into a compound unity."[7] Ihde observes that the hybridization of science and technology go in two different directions. The first is that science in our day is "fully" technoscience, meaning that science is now embodied materially within technology, suggesting that priority, ontologically, is given to technology over science. It may be described by saying that science serves at the pleasure of technology. Secondly, much of modern technology itself is technoscience. Ihde, as an example, refers to laser technology, which was only made possible by the scientific manipulation of photons. But "today the machines that scan grocery store bar codes, the reading of data from CDs to make music, and even my laser pointer all utilize the technologies that this type of science made possible. These are 'scientific' technologies now common in our lifeworld."[8] One may wish to focus on the benefits of technoscience, and legitimately so. Ricoeur, however, warns of the dangers, which must be viewed with an even more careful eye.

Ricoeur explains technoscience as analogous to the military-industrial complex. Essentially, his point is that the merging of technology and science creates much more far-reaching harm than had up until that point been possible (much like the military-industrial complex compounds the amount of harm and damage that warfare can do). Prior to technological extensions of science and technoscience "the range of human action was limited, and so the harms were also limited in space and time."[9] The chain of cause and effect between human action and its consequences becomes "foreshortened," meaning there is less mediation between the two. The result of this "abbreviation" is a massive and tragic widening of the range of horrid effects that follow human action.

When considered in the context of the ecological harm human action can cause in the world, technoscience would seem to refer to the employment of scientific research for its practical uses in technology to the end of manipulating and mastering nature for human advancement and survival. In other words, I take Ricoeur to mean the practice of science carried out, not for knowledge for its own sake, but intentionally for its technological uses for human ends. Technoscience for human advancement is easy enough to understand, but how is technoscience related to the idea of our survival?[10] The notion of survival is of extreme importance here, because the will to survive will be seen, with no small amount of irony, to be intertwined with the greatest threats to our extinction caused by our will to master nonhuman nature. It is the realization of the possibility of our own extinction, Ricoeur will contend, that demands ethical responsibility.

THE WILL TO SURVIVE AND ETHICAL RESPONSIBILITY: WHETHER TO BE AND HOW TO BE

There is a trajectory leading to ethical responsibility that begins with the mere instinctual drive to avoid death that exists in all organisms, after which it moves to the particularly human will to survive. But the will to survive results in attempts to master nature that ultimately lead to existential threats to human life. The ethical responsibility to which Hans Jonas and Ricoeur refer is the response we must have to threats in which human activity is implicated. However, a responsibility to ourselves does not oppose a responsibility to the planet and the nonhuman beings that dwell upon it. The crucial difference that must be recognized is that our dependence on the planet and its ecosystems is not equally reciprocated, much less of a partnership and far more the recognition of our absolute, necessary, and utter dependence on the planet on which we dwell. This in no way diminishes human worth or the legitimacy of our concerns, it simply acknowledges the reality of our own fragility in the larger picture (see chapter 4). Finally, it should be admitted that the threats to the planet that ultimately endanger our own survival are exacerbated by the fact that human activity long ago exceeded the drive to master nature merely for survival to a mastery of nature driven by the lust to dominate.

Ricoeur claims that with its focus on the evolution of species, Darwinian thinking "overlooked that a species is made up of individuals, none of which wants to die."[11] The "resistances to death" that reside in each individual (in biological forms such as our immune system) indicate a "pre-ethics," meaning that life "values itself as a good."[12] After all, the tenacity with which living organisms (humans included) strive to stay alive reveals that living is typically and instinctually understood to be preferable to ceasing to exist. Here, Ricoeur shifts the question from the instinctual to the cultural (more on the significance of this distinction in a moment). The question is not merely why there is something rather than nothing but, drawing on Hans Jonas, "Why there is something *of worth* rather than nothing?"[13] This not-so-subtle distinction is the difference between life's mere instinctual insistence on its own survival and why surviving matters—i.e., what is at stake is the kind of beings we choose to be. It is one thing to want to avoid death and quite another to consider living in a worthwhile manner.

Theodore George refers to this same distinction between the will to survive and how we are to be with even more depth and nuance. In developing a hermeneutical ethics, George notes Gadamer's (as well as novelist Milan Kundera's) reliance on Heidegger's proposition that "we are distinguished in our being by our concern for our own being."[14] As George says, we are distinguished in our being not in terms of the mere will to survive—*to* be—but more precisely *how* we shall be if we are to be. George is referencing a section early on in *Being and Time*. Within that same section, Heidegger says: "Dasein always understands itself in terms of its existence, in terms of its possibility to be itself or not to be itself."[15] What George calls the responsibility to understand (to interpret) as an ethical response to concrete situations, Ricoeur refers to a responsibility that "becomes the object of an ethics."[16] Beyond life's insistence on its *persistence*, ethics asks what our responsibilities are in our persisting. What is crucial to grasp here in light of the ecological crisis threatening human existence is that the concrete situation in which we find ourselves (ecological destruction) calls for an ethics that looks far forward. In Heideggerian terms, it calls forth the *possibilities* of our being (as what is *possible* has not yet come). A forward-looking ethics must include what Jonas has called the "heuristic of fear,"[17] explained in the following section, which Ricoeur finds necessary to address ecological catastrophe.

THE HEURISTIC OF FEAR AND THE
ETHICS OF THE FUTURE

To understand the heuristic of fear and why it is necessary, more must be said about the will to survive. Of all animals on the planet, human beings are the most ill-equipped with instinctual tools to survive. Ricoeur concurs with this Kantian observation and goes on to say that for human beings "culture takes the place of a certain instinctual void."[18] The instinct/culture dichotomy is essentially equivalent to the "nature/culture" dichotomy, which is typically understood to mean that the nonhuman world counts for "nature," and the human world counts for "culture." As many environmental philosophers and, especially, environmental anthropologists would point out, this divide is problematic on several levels.

The problem is not that nature and culture are different and can be distinguished one from the other. The recognition of a mere dichotomy is not the issue. The answer, then, to the problems of the nature/culture dualism is not to attempt to dissolve the difference. The real problem is to so radically separate one from the other that nature is subjugated to culture such that the former becomes a commodity to be used and exploited in the service of culture. Nature and culture so radically separated, interpreted as a great, uncrossable divide, is the product of a hyper-rationalist, and particularly Western, worldview. Nature and culture should neither be dissolved into one another nor radically separated as if in an irremediable conflict. Rather, the path forward relies on the recognition of both the difference and the complementary interrelation between them.

For an extensive treatment of the problems of the nature/culture dualism, I would refer the reader to a recent work by the anthropologist Philippe Descola, *Beyond Nature and Culture*,[19] and to several scholars in the literature of ecofeminism, notably Val Plumwood,[20] Karen Warren,[21] Noël Sturgeon,[22] and Donna Haraway.[23] Further, I would add Keith R. Peterson's observation of the work of the ecologist Paul Shepard. Peterson writes, "To his credit, Shepard rejects strong versions of the nature-culture dualism. He takes humans to be natural beings in need of cultural supplementation for survival and flourishing."[24] Peterson's account of Shepard echoes Ricoeur's account of culture filling an instinctual void.

Other animals within their habitats tend to adapt and thrive, setting aside the reality of predators and the dangers that all animals face in their habitats. The point is that nonhuman animals are genetically much better equipped to survive in "the wild." Human animals, while capable of surviving, lack those same instinctual tools and, therefore, have a far better chance at survival by employing particularly human technologies. From the time that human beings began to appear, it became necessary to develop technologies— e.g., learning to build fires, creating tools for hunting and gathering, onward through developing methods of agriculture, and irrigating rivers all served to enhance human life. As long as there have been humans there has been human manipulation of the nonhuman world (not to mention that all animals, to some degree, manipulate their environments in satisfying their basic needs).

Whether it was merely a matter of survival or, later on, to increase standards of comfortable living, human beings, it would seem hard to deny, have always sought to master nature in some form.

Perhaps we could understand "master" in its other meanings. For example, when we say an artist has mastered a musical instrument, we do not mean the artist is dominating or subjugating it. We mean that the artist has gained a high level of proficiency, a proficiency that requires the player to understand and conform to the rules of the instrument. Mastering nature can also be spoken of in two senses then. One, a form of mastery in which nature is understood as a lower order of being to be dominated, controlled, and exploited; the other, a more symbiotic form of mastery in which we become proficient in working with the ecological rules to which we must conform in order to thrive.

For tens of thousands of years, human activity for survival in their environment was largely inconsequential with regard to long-term, large-scale environmental harm. It has been in more modern times that human activity has been driving drastic environmental change, so much so that Paul Crutzen and Eugene Stoermer coined a new term for the current geological epoch, the "Anthropocene."[25] Although there has been some conflict of interpretation over precisely when the Anthropocene began or whether another term (such as "Capitalocene") might better describe the age,[26] it is generally agreed that we live in an age that is characterized by human activity as the major force behind changes to the Earth and its atmosphere and this threatens our survival. As Ricoeur remarked, there is "the fact that, for the first time, the attempts to master nature can lead to self-destruction. It is not evident that humanity will survive; it can do so, but only as a matter of will."[27] The "Anthropocene" has thrown this reality into sharp relief.

Here we have a grave irony. As a species ill-equipped to survive in nature, we adapted by mastering said nature. No longer subject to life in "the wild," we have homes with heating and cooling to give us relief from the bare elements, we drive on roads, fly in planes, and generally have little worry over predators in everyday living. Yet, it is precisely this attempted mastery over nature, which had its origins in the need to survive, that has become the cause of grave threats to the very survival we sought to secure! David Wood offers an apt description:

> Even if "in the last analysis" reproduction, nourishment, shelter, and survival are the most powerful forces, the realization of these fundamental goals in the context of human society gives rise to secondary goals—respect, power, wealth, knowledge, and freedom, which take on a life of their own, even if their primary role, so to speak, was to protect or enhance, or more surely secure, these basic ends. It would be a matter of critical concern if and when this second nature were to develop in such a way to threaten the satisfaction of basic biological needs.[28]

The secondary goals that Wood speaks of arise directly from basic, vital needs. But in another irony, the development and use of such secondary goals to maintain and even heighten these fundamental vital needs takes on a life of its own that works against these vital needs. Hence, the responsibility to make survival the object of an ethics becomes imperative. It is in this part of the interview that Ricoeur introduces Jonas's concept of the heuristic of fear.

Ricoeur summarizes the heuristic of fear as a "principle of discovery, a prospective view" that is "on the lookout for harms and dangers that are improbable but possible."[29] Rather than considering harms and dangers that are more likely to happen, the heuristic of fear bids us to also envision what could happen as a consequence of our actions, no matter how unlikely. We must wager that the improbable is nonetheless possible. Given the fact ecological collapse is not a fiction of some faraway dystopian future, the development and use of any technology that would contribute to and hasten such a collapse must imagine any possible deleterious outcome. What justifies such an approach? Would it not be wiser to consider the probable and not waste time with the far-fetched or highly implausible? There are two things I suggest that justify the heuristic of fear. The first, as noted just above, is that the effects of our attempts to master nature will likely result in our extinction if we fail to turn the tide. Moreover, the danger is not a minor harm easily correctable but a level of destruction that our best efforts cannot correct. And what could justify harms to sentient life, causing suffering in human and nonhuman animals that could be prevented in the first place? Such a view is a failure of solidarity, compassion, and empathy.

The second justification I propose for the heuristic of fear is already a part of Ricoeur's and Jonas's account of it. Namely, the current situation calls for us to look far into the future. The scale of the danger is indeed global, which refers to the degree of spatiality of harm's reach, but it is also related to time. The obligation to look far into the future (and to consider the consequences of even the improbable) arises from the fact that our actions now can have dire effects, not just for a brief and foreseeable time, but quite far beyond what we can conceive. As a "principle of discovery," the heuristic of fear becomes an orientation for how we consider outcomes. If we can conceive of a consequence that is possible, but seemingly unlikely, without the heuristic of fear, the attitude might well be "this seems improbable, so it is worth the risk." With the heuristic of fear, the attitude becomes "this seems improbable, but the probability alone is sufficient to move to avoid this outcome." The scale of potential harm should therefore eliminate any wager that a particular action is "worth" the risk.

The heuristic of fear begs the question, oft debated, of our obligation to future generations, that is, an obligation to that which does not yet exist. Here I offer just a few reflections. First, reconsider the primordial drive to live discussed above. As Ricoeur said, no member of any species wants to die. All organisms strive toward life and existence. Now, by referring again to the primordial will to survive, I do not intend to fall into the fallacy of deriving an *ought* from an *is*. An obligation to future generations is not derived from the mere existence of life and its striving to persist. It can just as well be argued that it may be better for the planet if humans did not exist in the future— i.e., an *ought* of human extinction from the *is* of human destruction of planetary life. The is/ought relationship can be shaky ground. David Wood ponders arguments for voluntary human extinction and observes one argument that draws this conclusion: "But might not the pursuit of something glorious be worth it even if it meant finally going down in the flames? Is not greatness attended by great risks?"[30] Here, there is no violation of rights as those who do not yet exist cannot be bearers of rights. Rather than deriving the *ought* of moral responsibility to future generations from the *is* of life's own attribution of merit to itself, could it not be that our responsibility to future generations lies within the scope and extent of the effects of our actions—i.e., our responsibility to the future comes from our ability to affect it? Capable human being is responsible human being.

Ricoeur also takes up the question of responsibility from Jonas in his 2005 book, *The Course of Recognition*. Ricoeur claims that Jonas, through the principle of responsibility is able to "remoralize" imputability on the juridical plane. Juridically, the agent is responsible for harm done, but it is on the moral plane where one is responsible for other persons. Within the scope of damage done lie those who are vulnerable and fragile. While Ricoeur notes that the idea of "future vulnerability of human beings and their environment" presents certain difficulties, he nonetheless says that as "far as our power extends [to cause harm], that far extend our capacities for harmful effects, and that far extends our responsibility for damage done."[31] Hence, due to the far-reaching effects of human action in a postindustrial world of technoscience, can we not say that we are indeed responsible for the extent of our power to do harm, even far into the future? Is there not a moral sense in which we do have responsibilities for persons who will be made vulnerable due to our actions? Ricoeur notes the difficulties with imputing "unlimited responsibility." In terms of penal law, for example, such unlimited responsibility becomes a kind of indifference in terms of penalties to the individual. The action must remain the "my own" of the agent that, Ricoeur fears, is overthrown by unlimited responsibility. Hence, he concludes:

> Between flight from responsibility and its consequences and the inflation to infinite responsibility, we must find a just measure and not allow the principle of responsibility to get too far from the initial concept of imputability and its obligation to make reparation or undergo punishment, within the limits of a relation

of spatial and temporal proximity between the circumstances of an action and its eventual harmful effects.[32]

A flight from responsibility can rightly be characterized in the assertion that "we are not responsible for those who do not yet exist" when it is reasonable to think that future generations *will exist* and will be subject to fragility and vulnerability precisely on account of our actions. Furthermore, future generations will be able to look back and impute guilt on past generations for their plight, just as the current generation does now. Thus: *If it is the case that future generations can look back and impute the guilt for their suffering on past generations, then present generations would seem to bear responsibility for generations yet to come to the extent that we can understand that the harmful effects of our actions will extend far beyond our time.* Culpability for our actions mitigated by ignorance would not seem to apply here insofar as it is the scientific consensus[33] that human action is causing irreversible damage to the planet.

There are two final considerations upon which to reflect in this section. The first is that we can understand why we should take future generations into consideration on the basis of a duty we have to existence itself. The second is that the question might be less one of a duty or obligation to future generations as one of what kind of people do we wish to be now, understood as concern for our own being. The second consideration is the answer and clarification to the first.

One might object to the premise that any duty to human existence exists. One might respond that duty to existence can only possibly be to actual existence not potential existence. How is the duty to future human existence any different than the claim that we have a duty to future generations? The difference is that by claiming that we have a duty to human existence, I am not claiming that the duty is to the existence to actual persons directly but rooted, rather, in that primordial drive to live. By affirming the ethical project of Jonas as an ethics of the future, that the will to survive means responsibility becomes an ethical project, it would seem that Ricoeur is proposing that the duty at hand is to do what is necessary to save our species from going over the precipice to extinction. Hence, the duty to "future generations" generates from an obligation to existence itself.

But, it can be quickly objected, human existence is not necessary, even for other ends. There is nothing on the planet at any level that actually depends upon human life for its own existence in any way that could be considered of necessity. Our dependence on the planet, by contrast, is entire, and utterly necessary. How can we claim an obligation to existence if our existence is in no way necessary? First, our existence may not be necessary, but the absence of necessity does not preclude a lack of moral obligation. Secondly, perhaps it is not a duty at all. Perhaps it is just a matter that it would be preferable if human life did endure than if it did not (assuming we learn to live symbiotically with the other-than-human world). Of course, this hinges on *how* we are to be if we *are* to be. The responsibility to be cannot mean to be at any cost or in any form. A responsibility *to be* would imply being in a way that is worthwhile. Moreover, given our absolute dependence upon the world that does not need us, it seems any future existence is beholden to living symbiotically with such a world. So perhaps a responsibility to future generations is, at heart, an outgrowth of a concern for our own being. The question might be more than "to be or not to be." Perhaps *to be and to be virtuously* is the better path. So, if we can get the *how to be* down, then we can justify why it is preferable that we endure. And if it is preferable to endure, better to endure, then perhaps the true obligation is simply to do the better thing rather than something lesser.

Placing our obligation to endure within the framework of preferability, we also avoid falling into the is/ought problem with which we might be charged. Above I mentioned that if we look at the *is* of the primordial will to survive as the source of the *ought* of our obligation to future generations, I am guilty of this fallacy. Is it not the case that simply shifting the *is* to a duty to existence itself, I am making the same error? If the obligation is understood as contingent, the is/ought problem can be avoided. *If* beyond the will to survive, we agree a concern for our own being is preferable, then it would seem to be the case that *if* we prefer to act out of our concern for our own being that we *ought* to conduct ourselves in certain ways that will preserve "nature" after us, meaning there will also be humanity after us. The obligation to future generations lies within the duty to existence, and the duty to existence is contingent upon whether we choose to have concern for our own being which, I argue, is preferable. In Kantian terms, I am making the obligation to future generations a hypothetical imperative rather than a categorical imperative. I am not saying that the obligation to future generations is not a categorical imperative (although that can be argued), I am simply saying I do not have to make it a categorical imperative. A hypothetical imperative is sufficient if it can be conceded that it is better to live in the now such that future generations can live and live well. Hence, the well-being of future generations is contingent upon how we choose to be, and if it is preferable to have a concern for our own being, then future generations are included within that concern.

As an addendum to this line of argumentation, a few words about future generations and current generations. There is no sharp divide between the present generation consisting of persons who exist now and persons who will come to be in the future. The future generation that comes to exist begins to exist in the milieu of the already presently existing generation that is in the process of passing out of existence. Therefore, in this overlap, if the human species passes into extinction, there will necessarily be a final generation.

What untold suffering and misery will befall that last generation of then already existing members of humanity? It is impossible to separate the thought of future generations from presently existing generations. Thus, any human action that would result in our extinction will necessarily, at that time, cause suffering to those who do exist. Any potential future generation that does not actualize will come at the expense of some then existing generation.

As we shall see in the next section, the aim to endure that means we must consider *how* we are to endure, and that "how" demands the recognition that without nonhuman nature there can be no human nature—i.e., if we destroy the Earth upon which we utterly depend, we cannot endure. This also means we must do better than what we have. In *Silent Spring*, Rachel Carson put it this way: "Have we fallen into a mesmerized state that makes us accept as inevitable that which is inferior or detrimental, as though having lost the will or the vision to demand that which is good?"[34] Carson insists that we have the "obligation to endure" and that in rightly understanding the effects of our choices on the planet we could endure well. In the next section, then, I will look at Ricoeur's considerations of the balance to be maintained between the feeling of being a part of nature with human "exceptionalism."

OTHER THAN NATURE OR A PART OF NATURE?

The question in the heading of this section is already a problem. What does it mean to ask if humans are a part of nature or nature is something exterior to human life? If we are a part of nature, what does that mean? If we are other than nature, what are we?[35] Environmentalists and environmental ethicists, especially, have struggled with the problem of the human relationship to nature and how it is we are a part of nature. Despite the philosophical difficulties with the term itself, Ricoeur provides a simple, yet insightful approach to the problem of our place in the overall ecosystem.

A term one often sees in the writings of environmental philosophers is "other-than-human nature" or "more-than-human-nature." I take the use of this term to express the idea that humans are a part of nature while speaking of other entities that are also a part of nature. This is helpful if we continue to use the term "nature" (which I suspect we will). If "nature" is a blanket term, it ought to include humans. The fact is that there is no "nature" per se, but upon the earth there are numerous distinguishable beings. We may refer to other-than-human nature because we, humans, are speaking. But, imaginatively, it would be the same from the perspective of other beings in the world if they were to conceptualize their surroundings—e.g., other-than-horse nature, other-than-tree nature, etc. In *Beyond Nature and Culture*, Descola cites a section of the poem "Keeper of Sheep" by Fernando Pessoa, which articulates this idea with the words: "I saw that there was no nature." The poem goes on to say that there are many different individual entities, such as "trees" or "stones," but that there is no "whole" called nature. At best, nature is "parts without a whole."[36] Any reference to "nature" is really a blanket term for collected, yet individual, parts.

Ricoeur articulated this idea differently but captures the heart of the matter well. We certainly find in Ricoeur an approach that aligns with what has been said in this section thus far. He also used the term "nature" but, as with Rachel Carson in 1962, using the term in 1993 is just as understandable. Ricoeur was responding to a question about a debate as to whether ecological thinking was anti-humanist. The interviewer refers to articles Ricoeur had written on Jonas where he had contended the principle of responsibility, when applied to the Earth and humans, was itself a humanist principle. Ricoeur responded:

> We must reconsider things on a more fundamental level. On the one hand, we are a part of nature; human beings must be set back in their place in the ecosystem: we are a fragment of the ecosystem, but the only fragment endowed with knowledge and responsibility. So, we have to balance the feeling of belonging to nature with the feeling of the exceptionalism of human beings in nature. This is a balance that continually has to be struck. When we reduce nature, as it were, to a quarry to be exploited, we violate the first principle, that of belonging to the ecosystem, but, on the other hand, in a naturalist ideology we forget that it is indeed human beings who raise questions. The capacity to question is, until proven otherwise, our privilege and our curse.[37]

Is Ricoeur falling into an egoistic anthropocentrism to refer to "human exceptionalism"? Taking his entire formulation here into account, there is no reason to take Ricoeur's choice of words as egoistically anthropocentric. In fact, in light of the way he frames his response, it would be an error to read "human exceptionalism" in this manner. Ricoeur is affirming here that human beings are both a part of nature (as a fragment of an overall ecosystem), but a fragment that is distinguished by certain capacities, such as the ability to question and the fact that we bear responsibility for what we know and how we act upon knowledge. Both principles—being a fragment of the ecosystem and being distinguished to varying degrees from other parts of it—must be held in a balance. If we take human exceptionalism as meaning a superiority by which we can reduce nature to a thing to be subjugated, the first principle is violated. So, the questions we raise and the responsibility we exercise cannot, in Ricoeur's framework, ever violate the fact of our belonging to the ecosystem. Ricoeur avoids both creating a hierarchical relationship of domination and dissolving the being of humans into some kind of "oneness" with nature. Instead, he insists on maintaining a creative tension between the two principles. Ricoeur is proposing a symbiosis rather than a relation of either domination or sameness.

Another way to understand that Ricoeur is not being egoistically anthropocentric is to acknowledge that all he is recognizing is what is different or unique about human beings. Our particular differences in no way provide a justification to exploit the nonhuman world in any destructive way. In Ricoeur's formulation, one might argue that our differences place upon us a unique burden of responsibility that places us to a great extent at the service of the ecosystem. So, the question of whether we are a part of nature or other than nature presents an either/or choice that should be framed as a both/and reality. Our responsibility lies in seeking wisdom on how we are that fragment and how we should conduct ourselves with those capacities that are unique to us. Indeed, if we are unique in our rational capacities, it seems evident that exercising those capacities in ways that will eventually destroy us demonstrates that we are not using those capacities very well! And what argument can be made that rationality entails a superiority that justifies the subjugation of supposed lower beings? It would seem, rather, that rationality enjoins us to exercise responsibility and care. We intuitively understand, for example, that a volcano is not culpable for CO_2 emissions resulting from an eruption because the volcano lacks knowledge, understanding, and agency. But we do hold *people* responsible for their actions precisely because they have knowledge, understanding, and agency. The rational capacities unique to human beings are more logically the wellspring of culpability rather than domination.

Elsewhere in the interview, Ricoeur says that the humanist project includes preserving nature. Based on Jonas's contention that an ethics of the future demands that we act such that human life will continue after our own time is gone, Ricoeur makes the simple statement, "Now, we know that for there to be humanity after us, there has to be nature after us; then, in this sense, the preservation of nature is part of the humanist project."[38] Addressing the ecological crisis is, for Ricoeur, a humanist endeavor. What Ricoeur's formula indicates, I would argue, is that any humanism that would subjugate ecology and any ecology that would be misanthropic is neither humanistic nor ecological. The humanistic and the other-than-human ecological must be balanced together for the flourishing of both. Naturally, what Ricoeur's point of view presumes is the acknowledgment that there are real environmental problems that threaten the future of human life on earth. Unfortunately, although widely acknowledged, this reality is not acknowledged universally (especially, for instance, with regard to climate change), which presents a political challenge in taking measures that must be taken. But how can anyone dispute the idea that the world we leave ought to be one in which persons can thrive and flourish? How can anyone dispute that a healthier planet means a healthier human race? It comes down to the question of concern for our own being. How do we best live and live well? And why not make the same attainable for those who are yet to come?

INTEGRATING ECOLOGY AND JUSTICE

Near the close of the interview, Ricoeur turns to the question of "ecology parties" and the possibility that they might integrate issues of justice into their platforms. Earlier on Ricoeur had taken note of the "general suspicion on the part of third world countries that our problems in advanced economies are being shifted to them."[39] He revisits that issue near the end by referencing the inequality between the global North and South in terms of distributive justice. Essentially, the heart of the environmental justice movement is about the intersection between social justice and environmental problems. While there are several aspects of environmental philosophy and ethics that can be separately considered from issues of social justice, a great insight of the environmental justice movement is that what is done to environments affects those who dwell within them, making environmental harm a matter of social justice. What affects our environment affects human life, not only our ability to survive, but our quality of life as well. We do not want a mere baseline of what is necessary for survival, we want to live and live well (which need not be construed as excess). So, Ricoeur asks whether the distribution of things like wealth and capital are ecological issues. The environmental justice movement answers with a resounding "yes"!

What sparked Ricoeur's revisiting of the ecology parties in France followed his observation that a "keen sense of respect, of love, and even veneration of nature is not exclusive of the human sense, for the point where the love of nature and the respect for human beings intersect, is suffering. As natural beings, we suffer."[40] Ricoeur refers to the "ethics of compassion" that is necessary due to the suffering humans have inflicted on other humans, but seems to suggest that the notion of suffering is what also links the concern (and love) that we have, or ought to have, for the environment. Environmental issues are ultimately political issues, in the truest sense of that word—i.e., having to do with the *polis*. After all, the gravest environmental threats that we face are created by social, political, and economic structures.

Ecology, Ricoeur continues in this section of the interview, must integrate its concerns into political systems that have to do with the distribution of power to as many people as possible. In a word: democracy. He refers to Hannah Arendt and her influence on his thinking here when he says we must return to a public use of reason—the forum.[41] And Ricoeur is careful not to limit the roles of professionals (scientists, ecologists, philosophers) as advisors to rulers but to be an "advisor to the public."[42] In terms of the ecological/environmental crisis both the planet and the polis must be integrated. If the polis fails to rise to the occasion of ensuring the planet does not perish, the polis itself will perish.[43] Ricoeur also strikes a careful equilibrium between the local and the global. Certain problems or decisions must be addressed at the local level. "What is better, to have a highway or a high-speed train in a certain area?"[44] However, potential harms that have a larger scope, especially global, must be so handled. The problem, Ricoeur laments, is that the scope of the danger requires international institutions that are truly empowered to address the danger, but no such institutions exist.[45] Chapter 5 will discuss the absolute necessity of such institutions for viable change.

CONCLUSION

While Paul Ricoeur was not an environmental philosopher in the sense that his formal philosophical work was addressed to environmental issues, what this interview demonstrates is that our global environmental crisis was of concern to Ricoeur and he did consider it with a philosophical mind, especially in the public role of the philosopher. Ricoeur's remarks and observations were in line with and relevant to most, if not all, of the debates within environmental philosophy at the time. It is the argument of this book, however, that it is in Ricoeur's philosophical work that we find novel ways of thinking about the environment and the content of environmental philosophy and ethics generally for now and the future.

NOTES

1. See note 1 in the introduction. All citations are from the English translation of the interview cited hereafter as Ricoeur, "Ethics, Politics, Ecology."

2. Environmental justice activists and thinkers tend to see issues of social justice and ecological/environmental crises as different sides of the same coin. While there can be distinct and separate issues, ultimately there is a connection between social and political justice and our responsibility to the environment.

3. Ricoeur, "Ethics, Politics, Ecology," 111.

4. Ricoeur, "Ethics, Politics, Ecology," 111.

5. Don Ihde, *Expanding Hermeneutics: Visualism in Science* (Evanston, IL: Northwestern University Press, 1998). See especially chapter 12, "Scientific Visualism."

6. Ricoeur, "Ethics, Politics, Ecology," 112.

7. Don Ihde, *Postphenomenology and Technoscience: The Peking Lectures* (Albany: SUNY Press, 2009), 41.

8. Ihde, *Postphenomenology and Technoscience*, 40 – 41.

9. Ricoeur, "Ethics, Politics, Ecology," 112.

10. One thinks here most prominently of "geo-engineering," also called "geo-constructivism," referring to the techno-scientific project of engineering the climate to ameliorate the negative effects of techno-science upon it.

11. Ricoeur, "Ethics, Politics, Ecology," 104.

12. Ricoeur, "Ethics, Politics, Ecology," 104.

13. Ricoeur, "Ethics, Politics, Ecology," 104. Emphasis original.

14. Theodore George, *The Responsibility to Understand: Hermeneutical Contours of the Ethical Life* (Edinburgh: Edinburgh University Press, 2020), ix.

15. Martin Heidegger, *Being and Time*, translated by Joan Stambaugh with revisions by Dennis J. Schmidt (Albany: SUNY Press, 2010).

16. Ricoeur, "Ethics, Politics, Ecology," 104.

17. See Hans Jonas, *The Imperative of Responsibility: In Search of an Ethics for the Technological Age*, translated by Hans Jonas with the Collaboration of David Herr (Chicago: University of Chicago Press, 1984), especially pages 26–27 and 202–3.

18. Ricoeur, "Ethics, Politics, Ecology," 104.

19. Philippe Descola, *Beyond Nature and Culture*, translated by Janet Lloyd (Chicago: University of Chicago Press, 2013).

20. See Plumwood's *Feminism and the Mastery of Nature* (London: Routledge, 1993). Plumwood's discussion of dualisms in chapter 2 is particularly insightful. Also, see her *Environmental Culture: The Ecological Crisis of Reason* (London: Routledge, 2002).

21. Karen J. Warren, *Ecofeminist Philosophy: A Western Perspective on What It Is and Why It Matters* (Lanham, MD: Rowman & Littlefield, 2000).

22. Noël Sturgeon, *Ecofeminist Natures: Race, Gender, Feminist Theory and Political Action* (New York: Routledge, 1997).

23. Donna Haraway, *The Companion Species Manifesto: Dogs, People, and Significant Otherness* (Chicago: Prickly Paradigm Press, 2003).

24. Keith R. Petersen, *A World Not Made for Us: Topics in Critical Environmental Philosophy* (Albany: SUNY Press, 2020), 43.

25. See Paul J. Crutzen and Eugene F. Stoermer, "The Anthropocene," *Global Change Newsletter* 41 (2000): 17–18.

26. See, *Anthropocene or Capitalocene: Nature, History, and the Crisis of Capitalism*, edited by Jason W. Moore (Oakland: PM Press, 2016. For a brief discussion of the conflict of intepretations between these two terms, see David Utsler and Cynthia Nielsen, "(Environmental) Hermeneutics at the Heart of the Anthropocene: Ricoeurian and Gadamerian Perspectives," in *Analecta Hermeneutica* 13 (2021): 52–72 (especially 55–57).

27. Ricoeur, "Ethics, Politics, Ecology," 104.

28. David Wood, *Reoccupy Earth: Notes toward an Other Beginning* (New York: Fordham University Press, 2019), 203.

29. Ricoeur, "Ethics, Politics, Ecology," 105.

30. Wood, *Reoccupy Earth*, 209.

31. Paul Ricoeur, *The Course of Recognition*, translated by David Pellauer (Cambridge, MA: Harvard University Press, 2005). 108–9.

32. Ricoeur, *The Course of Recognition*, 109.

33. See, for example, International Panel on Climate Change, *Climate Change 2022: Impacts, Adaptation and Vulnerability* (2022). The summary volume of this report can be found at https://www.ipcc.ch/report/ar6/wg2/downloads/report/IPCC _AR6_WGII_SummaryVolume.pdf.

34. Rachel Carson, *Silent Spring*, 50th Anniversary Edition (Boston: Mariner Books, 2002), 12.

35. Cf. David Utsler, "Is Nature Natural? And Other Linguistic Conundrums: Scott Cameron's Hermeneutic Defense of the Concept of Nature," in *Environmental Philosophy* 15, no. 1 (Spring 2018): 77–89.

36. Descola, *Beyond Nature and Culture*, 1.

37. Ricoeur, "Ethics, Politics, Ecology," 113.

38. Ricoeur, "Ethics, Politics, Ecology,"114.

39. Ricoeur, "Ethics, Politics, Ecology,"106.

40. Ricoeur, "Ethics, Politics, Ecology,"115.

41. See Ricoeur, "Ethics, Politics, Ecology," 108.

42. Ricoeur, "Ethics, Politics, Ecology,"108.

43. See a different interview in the same volume, "The *Polis* is Fundamentally Perishable—Its Survival Depends on Us," in Paul Ricoeur, *Philosophy, Ethics, & Politics*, translated by Kathleen Blamey (Cambridge, UK: Polity Press, 2020), 37–44.

44. Ricoeur, "Ethics, Politics, Ecology," 110.

45. See Ricoeur, "Ethics, Politics, Ecology," 105.

Chapter 2

Environmental Identity
in the Flesh

Corporeality in Environmental Selfhood

The concept of environmental identity must be at the heart of any herme-neutic account of environmental thought. Both Ricoeur and Gadamer taught that the act of interpretation was always also an interpretation of the self. The way in which something is understood reflects something of the one who understands. How one understands says something about the disposition and character of the interpreter. Yet, interpretation also has the dynamic of exposing the interpreter to something new, something that is transformative and constitutes the ever-changing self in new ways. In terms of environmen-tal identity, it could be said that in one sense, all identity is environmental identity. If identity and selfhood is in part constituted by the Other, then it is always the entities and objects exterior to me (those which *environ* me) that form and shape who I am. Environmental identity can be understood in a very broad way to include any kind of environs—architecture, cities, etc. For the purposes of environmental hermeneutics and environmental philosophy in the present inquiry, which is concerned with keeping the planet (and therefore ourselves) from destruction, environmental identity is concerned with how the formation of the self orients us to act in ways that are either beneficial for a sustainable environment or exploitive of it.

A Ricoeurian approach to environmental identity springs from what he referred to as the three philosophical intentions of his book *Oneself as Another*.[1] I have published previously discussing these three intentions as the basis for a hermeneutical approach to environmental identity.[2] I will revisit that foundation briefly before going on to focus on the corporeal nature of environmental identity and how a "fleshly" approach to environmental iden-tity is the key to overcoming alienation from what I will frequently refer to as "earth-nature."

ENVIRONMENTAL IDENTITY—A
RICOEURIAN APPROACH

Environmental identities, it seems obvious enough, are identities related to space and place—i.e., that which environs us. We grow a sense of self from the things around us by how were relate to them, perceive them, and what meanings they hold for us. At one level, one could refer to "place identity" as well as environmental identity. So, when we speak of an environmental identity, generally, we are referring to the sense of self and how one interprets one's being-in-the-world in and with the space and place within which one dwells. As with the notion of identity itself, environmental identity is complex and multidimensional. One's sense of self can be in relation to more immediate environments (e.g., one's home, the geographical location in which one dwells, etc.), but the sense of self and self-understanding can also be in relation to larger or more remote environments, especially the earth itself—what we might think of as our common home. This latter is especially true due to phenomena such as climate change. Planetwide events now affect us, and technology has made the world significantly smaller, meaning our self-reflection occurs on a global scale.

Three Philosophical Intentions

Ricoeur's most extensive study of selfhood, the crowning achievement of his philosophical anthropology, is no doubt his *Oneself as Another*. He begins the introduction to that work by referring to "the point of convergence between the three philosophical intentions that influenced the preparation of the studies that make up this book."[3] It is here that I find a strong foundation to formulate a hermeneutical concept of environmental identity. The point of convergence between these three intentions are designated, Ricoeur says, by the title of the book itself. The title *Oneself as Another* indicates that selfhood is constituted by way of relation to another. The question for environmental hermeneutics is whether that "other" can be an environment (or more precisely, the members or individual entities of that environment). Ricoeur seems to imply as much when he describes the Other as polysemic. This polysemy of the Other, he says, implies that the Other is not to be reduced merely to the otherness of another person.[4] While Ricoeur does not say whether the environment is a nonhuman other, I think the overall character of the work indicates that no Other can be excluded that, in dialectic with the self, could potentially be constitutive of identity. Earlier, he had said that the question "who?" is always answered through the detour of the question "what?," so much so that "the being of the world is the necessary correlate to the being of the self."[5] There is no world, he says, without a self within it and so self without a world in which one can act. Certainly, this world as a whole is made up of many particulars, many of which are members other-than-human nature that are constitutive of identity. With this in mind, let us briefly consider the three philosophical intentions of the book in terms of environmental identity.

The First Intention

The first intention is related to the Cartesian cogito, in which the subject is posited directly and immediately. "I think, therefore, I am." Ricoeur objects, however, that the self only knows itself indirectly within reflective meditation through detours. What are detours? Language, cultural signs and symbols, experiences, relationships, etc. The cogito can only posit *that* I am, not *who* I am in any robust sense as selfhood and identity. Descartes's project, especially in the first two Meditations, was to seek something of which he could be certain, that which could not be doubted. Proceeding by way of doubt, he concluded that his existence could not be doubted, even if he was deceived, insofar as to be deceived is predicated on existing. That he exists now raises the question as to *what* this existing thing is. Descartes concludes that he is no more than a thinking thing. He is a mind, an intellect. The immediate positing of the subject in the cogito can only say *that* he is and *what* he is (i.e., a "disembodied thinking thing"). Certainly, *what* we are is far more than just intellect and rationality, but for Descartes anything outside the mind can be doubted and, therefore, any question of *what* cannot be entertained outside the mind.

But what Descartes cannot answer is the question of *who* I am. *That* I am, yes. *What* I am (no matter how incomplete), yes. But *who* I am cannot be reached in the Cartesian cogito. *Who* thinks, doubts, is deceived, and so on can only be *identified* via what Ricoeur describes as "the indirect approach of reflection through the detour of analysis."[6] While we may be "thinking things," we have to think *about* something. The relation of environmental identity to this first philosophical intention is simply that included in the things we think about is the environment. To be serious about one's environmental identity is to think reflectively, to analyze one's relationship to the environment and the sense of self that derives from that relationship. In sum, it is to live the examined life—examined as a citizen or member of the earth. In *The Gay Science*, Nietzsche wrote: "We do not belong to those who only get their thoughts from books, or at the prompting of books,—it is our custom to think in the open air, walking, leaping, climbing, or dancing on lonesome mountains by preference, or close to the sea, where even the paths become thoughtful."[7] Nietzsche here is talking about the importance of thinking not only with the words of others in books, but out in the world itself. Placed in the context of environmental identity, we must get our thoughts about ourselves by being in the "open air." Environmental identity is no mere abstract reflection or an inner psychology, it is constituted by "walking, leaping, climbing, or dancing" in encounters with the other-than-human world.

The Second Intention

The second intention identifies two "major meanings" of identity marked by the Latin terms—*idem* and *ipse*. *Idem* (sameness) refers to the unchanging permanence over time of the individual whereas *ipse*, in contrast to an unchanging inner core, refers to the recognition of the self over time and change, which Ricoeur explicitly associates with selfhood. "Selfhood," I take to be in Ricoeur's thought, to be associated with the plurality of difference that comes to constitute identity. What is identity? Permanence in time? Change and variability? For Ricoeur, it is a matter of the dialectic between the two. Because *ipse* refers to change over time, Ricoeur finds a connection to the function of narrative "which reconciles the same categories Locke took as contraries: identity and diversity."[8] Selfhood emerges as same and diverse in a lifelong dialectic between that which is identifiable over time and the inevitable change that comes over a life.

What do *idem* and *ipse* provide our conception of environmental identity? Essentially, that one's environmental identity is not fixed and static over time, but always subject to change and development. This is a crucial point for the reason that an environmental identity can change for the better—i.e., we can change our story. Environmental identity, on this Ricoeurian account, is something that must be constantly engaged. We might say that environmental identity must constantly expose itself to one of those fundamental gestures of philosophy, namely, to examine oneself. The hope that this offers is that both individual environmental identities and, more importantly, the collective environmental identity of humankind can turn the tide. Whether that will happen or the likelihood that it will is another matter, but the possibility is reason to continue to work for a healthy planet.

The Third Intention

This third intention, Ricoeur says, "crowns the first two dialectics."[9] In the second intention/dialectic, identity as *ipse* is certainly related to the other. This relation is characterized as change, variation, and development over time with that which is exterior. Ricoeur characterizes this relation of the same to the other in terms of the individual being *alongside* the other in the form of comparison. But this third intention is richer and more profound where selfhood is constituted by the other and one's selfhood "implies otherness to such an intimate degree that one cannot be thought of with the other, that instead one passes into the other."[10] Beyond merely resonating with the other, there is a greater intimacy at work here where one is oneself only to the extent that one is other.

As Ricoeur develops this in later chapters of *Oneself as Another* (especially chapters 7–9), this third intention is revelatory of an ethics. He says that this crown of the previous dialectics is most fully developed as an ethics and morality where the "*autonomy* of the self will appear then to be tightly bound up with *solicitude* for one's neighbor and with *justice* for each individual."[11] This suggests that the self is only fully the self, flourishing and thriving, as a self whose concern for its own being is demonstrated in concern for the other. Solicitude need not be limited to solicitude for other persons, but other-than-human others as well. As noted above, the polysemic character of otherness indicates that the "other" does not refer only to other persons. Also, in light of our asymmetric dependence upon the earth (see chapter 4), solicitude for the earth and the environment that necessarily sustains human life becomes a part of the humanist project that was discussed in the first chapter. What I now argue is that each intention and every aspect of identity is realized as an environmental identity in the flesh.

THE CORPOREALITY OF ENVIRONMENTAL IDENTITY

In the tenth and final study in *Oneself as Another*, "What Ontology in View?," Ricoeur wants to explore the *being* of the self. He asks "what sort of being or entity" is the self?[12] While the previous chapters were grouped distinctly under one of the three philosophical intentions that make up the book overall, Ricoeur says that in the tenth study on the ontology of the self, all three intentions will serve as guide to his ontological considerations. By the time he gets to the third intention—the dialectic between selfhood and otherness—he points out this last is more fundamental than the first two. It is in this section of the study that he introduces the importance of the body—the flesh. Ricoeur's "exploration" demonstrates, I argue here, that environmental identity (or what we might call "environmental selfhood") is an enfleshed identity.

Richard Kearney has provided a most useful and succinct account of Ricoeur's early "phenomenology of the flesh," his turn to the text, and his return to the body and a "hermeneutics of the flesh" in the article, "Between Flesh and Text: Ricoeur's Carnal Hermeneutics."[13] In his early work in *Freedom and Nature: The Voluntary and the Involuntary*,[14] Ricoeur provided a "diagnostic of the body" in the form of an "incarnate cogito," wherein resided a dialectic between the voluntary and the involuntary. Kearney then recounts that Ricoeur regrettably abandoned the project of a phenomenology of the body as he turned to a hermeneutics of the text. Even more regrettably, this textual turn was not simply an abandonment of this project, but at times Ricoeur opposed the text to flesh, granting a place of privilege to the text over the flesh. The flesh has more of an "immediacy," whereas language offers distance and reflection, which would be place of interpretation. Thankfully, however, Kearney highlights Ricoeur's return to the flesh and the body as a locus of interpretation in *Oneself as Another*. What this return to the body provides for a Ricoeurian account of environmental identity is to be found primarily in Ricoeur's account of passivity and the flesh as mediator.

Before turning to passivity, I wish to briefly explain why I am arguing for the corporeality of environmental identity, which is to say why I think environmental identity is fundamentally a matter of the flesh. "Our most fundamental sense of ourselves is our body."[15] These words from Kearney are descriptive of the Ricoeurian incarnate cogito, or embodied cogito. Whatever sense of ourselves we have in the mind is almost always mediated through the body, for it is in the body that we experience the world. In infancy, our first sense of ourselves comes through touch and taste. A child feeding at the breast of its mother or being held and caressed begins to know itself and its world in tactile ways long before the conceptualization of these things in language. Even after we develop our rational capacities, we never cease to come into contact with the world through the body and interpret ourselves in that world.

Identity, generally, is largely constituted by what is exterior to us. Environmental identity, it follows, is constituted in relation to the physical environment in which we dwell. Any abstractions about environmental identity that are drawn out of our contact with our physical environment are necessarily predicated on physical contact with it. Further, it must be insisted that an environmental identity is determined by *how* we touch our environment. In his much-celebrated *Last Child in the Woods*, Richard Louv writes of "nature-deficit disorder" in children (and adults). Louv argues that the "healthy development" of the senses requires direct contact with nature.[16] "Nature," in this context, refers to the outdoors—dirt, trees, rivers and streams, and such. The more we lack this direct contact the more stunted our sensory life becomes. I would argue our environmental identity is stunted as well at great cost, not only to us, but to the environment also. To be alienated from the other-than-human world ultimately tends to a kind of alienation from the self.

Ricoeur provides what he calls a "triad of passivity," the first of which he describes as "the passivity represented by the experience of one's own body—or better, as we shall say later, of the *flesh*—as the mediator between the self and a world which is itself taken in accordance with its variable degrees of practicability and so of foreignness."[17] Ricoeur speaks of varying degrees of passivity at work in this first kind of passivity that reveal one's body "to be the mediator between the intimacy of the self and the externality of the world."[18] The first of these varying degrees of passivity is of primary interest here with regard to environmental identity. In one's own body one experiences the resistance of other bodies. Although a kind of passivity, it occurs in active touching. For Ricoeur's purposes, he simply wants to say that the resistance from external bodies attests to their existence and our own. Passivity also implies a receptivity in which the body is acted upon and the external world is received, as it were, into the intimacy of my own world, becoming a source of the very constitution of the self.

This is an important point requiring that the distinction between the second intention (the dialectic of *idem* and *ipse*) and the third intention (the dialectic of the self and the other than self) be highlighted. The second intention, Ricoeur notes, "maintains a preeminently disjunctive character," that is to say, in the dialectic of *idem* and *ipse*, the two poles remain distinct. This distinction is necessary for *idem* and *ipse* to fulfill their function as a narrative constitution of the self. However, it is in the third intention in which same passes through the other in such intimacy that one is oneself insofar as one is other. So, in this way "otherness is not added on to selfhood from outside, as though to prevent its solipsistic drift, but that it belongs instead to the tenor of meaning and to the ontological constitution of selfhood,"[19] which is what most distinguishes the third intention from the second. The importance of this for environmental identity (and environmental philosophy) cannot be overstated. What I am arguing for in this chapter is no less than an ontological constitution of selfhood by interpreting earth-nature[20] as another self and oneself as earth-nature.

With these considerations in mind, I would now like to return to Ricoeur's claim that in passivity the body is what mediates the intimacy of the self and the external world. When we place our focus to that part of the external world we call earth, we understand that it is in the body that what I am calling "earth-nature" is understood as a part of us and we are a part of it. Earth-nature is oneself and one's other-than-self. Referring back to chapter 1, we are at once a fragment of the ecosystem and distinct within it (incidentally, as is every other part). Here one experiences a sense of intersubjectivity with other-than-human nature that becomes constitutive of selfhood as such. The reference to intersubjectivity is not, however, without its difficulties. Can we truly speak of an intersubjectivity with trees and dirt and oceans and rivers? Are we not in danger of merely projecting ourselves onto other-than-human nature, putting words in its mouth, so to (anthropomorphically) speak?

On one hand, we have what Steven Vogel refers to as the "silence of nature."[21] In the traditional sense that a speaker implies and hearer, and that the speaker is also a hearer and vice versa, we cannot say that nature speaks and that we can engage in a process of the exchange of thoughts, feelings, needs, and desires, at least not as we do so with other human beings with who we have a shared language. Even with other people, there are barriers to understanding due to our finitude and the limitations of shared experiences. But at least with other people, we can "exchange stories"[22] or narrate our lives to one another with the hope of overcoming the lack of understanding in order to achieve mutual understanding. The fact remains still that even between our own species with a shared language, we exist in a sort of post-Babel reality where, as Donatella Di Cesare says, we are "exiled in language."[23] The best we can do is engage in what Ricoeur calls "linguistic hospitality"[24] in which we welcome the stranger and risk the possibility of understanding. If intersubjectivity has its limits even within the same species and a shared language community, how can we even begin to speak of intersubjectivity with other-than-human nature?

On the other hand, there is Gadamer's famous line in *Truth and Method*, "Being that can be understood is language," after which he noted that "interpretation" is our relation to other beings. Then he wrote, "Thus we speak not only of a language of art but also of a language of nature—in short, of any language that things have."[25] Gadamer's words would seem to suggest that language is broadly defined as the means by which being discloses itself, whatever that means may be. More to the point, when any being discloses itself in its being, this is in some broad sense, language. This would likewise imply that the one to whom being is disclosed understands when the disclosure is "translated" into one's own language. But does Gadamer thereby avoid the problem of the "silence of nature" that Vogel insists upon? How can we avoid making the mistake that what we believe other-than-human nature is disclosing to us is none other than what it is we have constructed and imposed upon it?

There are two ways, hermeneutically, that Vogel's "silence of nature" and Gadamer's "being that can be understood is language" (even the language of nature) could be mediated. The first would simply acknowledge that even if nature is silent in terms of human language, that does not imply that nothing of nature can be understood. The "being of nature" still has disclosure. The second mediation is the prelinguistic corporeal "touch" with nature, wherein the flesh mediates the intimacy of the self with the externality of the world, and from which we can translate into our own language the experience itself. Both mediations are joined in the principle that other-than-human nature can be understood (and rightly) despite the dissimilarities (in kind not just degree) between humans and other-than-human nature. And in the context of this chapter, which is focused on environmental identity, the mediation of human being with other-than-human nature becomes the "ground" from which environmental identity grows.

The first mediation springs from the finitude of understanding, which implies only the limits of finitude, not the impossibility of understanding some things. In other words, that the totality of a being cannot be comprehended does not mean that we cannot have some genuine understanding of that being. While the finitude of understanding fellow human beings cannot be conflated with the finite understanding of other-than-human being, it would be wrong to think the "silence of nature" implies nothing of nature can be understood (and I think that Vogel would agree with this statement). Despite the silence of nature in terms of human speech (and, therefore, conversation), nature is not simply a blank slate upon which we write. Other-than-human nature imposes itself upon our passivity. Keith Peterson rightly observed that the human mind and body depend upon other-than-human nature to provide not only the content of our thought but the form of thought as well (see chapter 4, note 7). Nature constitutes us, we do not constitute it, at least in its own being. The only way we as *human beings* constitute nature is in terms of what it might mean *to us* in various contexts of our lived experience. That is, in our relationship to that which is not human. Or more accurately, all of those differentiated things that are not human.

We must understand other-than-human nature, to the extent that we can, on its own terms. Of course, "terms" is already revelatory of our finitude in that the only way that we can think of understanding other-than-human-nature (even to the extent we seek to understand it as it is in itself apart from our valuing of it) is with a linguistic reference, despite nature's linguistic silence. While Vogel may indeed be correct in what he means by nature's silence, as language-beings we seem unable to situate our understanding in anything other than language. So, the mediation in question would consist in recognizing the tension between two poles: on one hand, while nature is silent with regard to speaking for itself as humans speak and, therefore, we must be cautious not to "put words in the mouth of nature," there is the other hand where what can rightfully be understood of nature can only be understood by us with the language that we speak. Our agenda must be to learn how to speak to each other, and what we speak about is the planet upon which we dwell and rely upon for existence. Kearney and Fitzpatrick summarize this sentiment in their words "that the looming ecological crisis reveals and unprecedented call for international collaboration—narrative hospitality, cooperative conversation—grounded in the understanding that, in relation to our earth, we (all of earth's diverse inhabitants) are one community."[26] As Ricoeur would say, we are a distinct fragment of the ecosystem and simultaneously one with the ecosystem.

How can we say that the "silence of nature" and Gadamer's "language of nature" can be mediated by the flesh? Is it possible, in terms of the third philosophical intention of *Oneself as Another*, to meaningfully "pass through" the other of other-than-human nature such that I am constituted in my environmental identity, especially in the flesh, by way of that intimacy? What benefit is a "language of nature" (if there is such a thing) if nature yet remains silent? My argument here, based on Ricoeur's hermeneutics of the flesh, is that with regard to other-than-human nature, or what I referred to above as "earth-nature," it is in tactile contact, an intimacy with "earth-other" that we are constituted in our environmental identity. Nature may remain silent as regards human language, but it is the body, the flesh, that mediates external earth-nature to the intimacy of the self. While it is true that a central feature of hermeneutics is dialogue (which can presumably happen, except in a metaphorical sense, only between language beings), hermeneutics is fundamentally about interpretation, that is, understanding. In explaining his intention by the phrase "Being that can be understood is language," Gadamer said, "The principle of hermeneutics simply means that we should try to understand everything that can be understood."[27]

Regarding the universality of hermeneutics, Gadamer states:

> The universality of the hermeneutical perspective is all-encompassing. I once formulated this idea by saying that being that can be understood is language. This is certainly not a metaphysical assertion. Instead, it describes, from the *medium of understanding*, the unrestricted scope possessed by the hermeneutical perspective. It would be easy to show that all historical experience satisfies this proposition, *as does the experience of nature.*[28]

If Gadamer's assertion is that being can be understood as language is correct and that hermeneutical experience is universal, the "medium of understanding" with regard to the experience of nature is at first prelinguistic, namely, the flesh. Only after does the medium of understanding become language. Understanding earth-nature, because it is corporeal, requires corporeal interaction if we are to be constituted in a healthy environmental identity that will in turn orient human action to turn the tide of environmental destruction. If we are to have an "ethics of responsibility" toward the earth, we have to learn to touch it.

I have not truly answered the specific question of whether intersubjectivity is possible between humans and nonhuman others, and I will leave it unanswered here. Suffice it to say that intersubjectivity requires at least two *subjects*. That seems evident enough. But is it possible that what we are calling intersubjectivity indicates something we are aiming at that, while it may not be properly called *intersubjectivity*, is some sort of interrelation with the other-than-human world that is not reducible to meanings we impose upon that world from without? Can the receptive passivity Ricoeur speaks of be the space in which we receive other-than-human nature on its own "terms," that then grounds our active agency within those terms?[29] Also, further distinctions would be necessary in a discussion on intersubjectivity, such as that which occurs between humans and other animals. For we cannot speak of intersubjectivity with "nature" as a whole, but of all the varied members that make up the parts without a whole.[30]

Finally, passivity, furthermore, "grounds" the ability to act. Ricoeur writes, "The fact that the flesh is most originally mine and of all things that which is closest, that its aptitude for feeling is revealed most characteristically in the sense of touch . . . these primordial features make it possible for the flesh to be the organ of desire, the support for free movement" so, therefore, the "flesh is the place of all passive syntheses on which the active syntheses are constructed."[31] Or, as Ricoeur wrote in *Time and Narrative*, "It is on the ground of such a philosophy of the flesh that the 'I can' can be thought. The flesh, in this sense, is the coherent ensemble of my powers and nonpowers."[32] The importance of this analysis for environmental identity cannot be overstated. It must be kept in mind that it is not a question as to whether each of us has an environmental identity, but in what direction (sense) it is "cultivated" (if I may use another "earthy" metaphor) in our activity. Richard Kearney writes:

> Clearly, the current generation is becoming increasingly dependent on electronic devices that connect them with virtual worlds while disconnecting them from real ones. At the touch of a tab, we gain a digital universe but lose touch with ourselves. We create virtual profiles at the price of tactile experience. Omnipresent access as the cost of real presence.[33]

Kearney here is referring to the phenomenon he calls "excarnation," a term which he uses to describe how we have lost "touch" with touch. The reclamation of touch (anacarnation[34]) is necessary in order to cultivate one's environmental identity, without which we become alienated both from ourselves in our own bodies as well as the earth and the bodies that dwell upon it. It is the task of environmental hermeneutics to overcome this dual alienation.

ENVIRONMENTAL IDENTITY AND
THE HERMENEUTICAL TASK OF
OVERCOMING ALIENATION

Ricoeur (as well as Gadamer) considered hermeneutics to aim at overcoming distance and, in doing so, for one to understand oneself. Ricoeur wrote that the "deepest wish of hermeneutics" is to understand that "all interpretation is to conquer a remoteness."[35] Ricoeur here refers to the remoteness between a past time from which a text comes and the one interpreting it, but I would contend that the hermeneutical task of overcoming remoteness applies, not only to historical times of which we did not live (and the texts of those times), but of anything that can be described as unfamiliar, strange, or not understood. And, as Gadamer said, noted just above, hermeneutics aims at understanding everything that is possible to understand. Everything, in Gadamer's formulation, that is not understood would be considered alien or unfamiliar, but the hermeneutical task is to "venture into the alien, the lifting up of something out of the alien, and thus the broadening and enrichment of our own experience of the world."[36] It is then, in conquering a remoteness, an unfamiliarity, that the interpreter experiences "the growth of his own understanding of himself that he pursues through his understanding of the other."[37] When that other is an environment, then the self-understanding that results in environmental in nature and, hence, an environmental identity. What does it mean to be alienated from our environment and what does that mean in relation to environmental identity?

Pediatric occupational therapist Angela J. Hanscom wrote that it is first through touch that children learn both about themselves and the world around them. It is in the encounter with the Other of the environing world that, from the very beginning of life, one's sense of self is constituted. At first, however, Hanscom says that in the early stages of development that the "brain has not learned to differentiate one spot from another"[38] when children first experience touch. Hanscom observed that children begin to learn about themselves from contact with the world around them the more they are exposed to "tactile experiences." The ability to discern and discriminate between "bodies," so to speak, comes from more and greater contact with one's environment. There is no reason to think that the maintenance of healthy brain development (and overall physical development) can do without continued touch throughout life with what I have referred to in this chapter as "earth-nature." As Hanscom would confirm, the active and continued use of the senses must be maintained. Touch does not stop after a certain stage of development.

Richard Louv, who coined the term "nature-deficit disorder," referred to above, also coined the term "Nature Principle." Louv writes, "Primarily a statement of philosophy, the Nature Principle is supported by a growing body of theoretical, anecdotal, and empirical research that describes the restorative power of nature—its impact on our intelligence; on our physical, psychological, and spiritual health; and on the bonds of family, friendship and the multi-species community."[39] Everything Louv lists here are among the many things that constitute identity. Insofar as each of these things that constitute our identity are impacted by our corporeal connection to earth-nature, it is rightly argued that the cultivation of environmental identity is crucial to our overall sense of self and our right relation to all aspects of the world around us. Overcoming the alienation from earth-nature (coextensive with alienation from vital life) in the age of technology and "excarnation" becomes an important task of environmental hermeneutics.

Returning now to the quote from the first paragraph in this section, Ricoeur said that all interpretation is intended to overcome remoteness. In terms of the distance of the "past cultural epoch to which the text belongs and the interpreter," Ricoeur said that by

> overcoming this distance, by making himself contemporary with the text, the exegete can appropriate its meaning to himself: foreign, he makes it familiar, that is he makes it his own. It is thus the growth of his own understanding of himself that he pursues through his understanding of the other. Every hermeneutics is thus, explicitly or implicitly, self-understanding by means of understanding others.[40]

Is it possible now to take this notion of overcoming distance that Ricoeur speaks of in terms of the interpretation of a text and place it in the context of Ricoeur's later hermeneutics of the flesh? Furthermore, can this be done without simply turning the environment into a kind of quasi-text?[41] It is amply clear, I contend, that philosophical hermeneutics is about understanding and, as Gadamer said, understanding everything that can be understood. A text from an earlier historical epoch is but one thing to understand. In fact, it is less the text that we seek to understand as the historical epoch from which we are distanced (what Ricoeur would call the "world of the text"). The text, in this case, should be considered the medium through which the historical epoch is interpreted. The text mediates (brings near) a remote time to the present world of the interpreter. What if, I propose, not succumbing to the "metaphor of the text," we consider what it means for the text and flesh to be medium? For interpretation must be understood as meaning in the "in-between," that space between the interpreter and that which is interpreted, the distance between which we seek to overcome. While the text is the proper medium between an interpreter and history, it is the flesh that is the proper medium between a self and environment. Moreover, the distance (or alienation) between an interpreter and history is time, whereas the distance and alienation between an interpreter and an environment is the excarnation of the flesh from vital contact with earth-nature. Flesh and excarnation are not merely some metaphorical types of text and time, but merely characteristic of *media* involved in the act of interpretation. Therefore, if the text "is the very *medium* within which we can understand ourselves,"[42] with regard to the interpretation of historical epochs, the flesh, then, is the very medium within which we can understand ourselves with regard to environments—i.e., environmental identity! There is no metaphor of the text at work here with flesh.

The flesh is medium, period. Carnal and environmental hermeneutics intersect in environmental identity.

CONCLUSION

This chapter represents a first gesture toward what I hope to become further explorations into the place and importance of philosophical hermeneutics in addressing the precarious threat of ecological doom. Whether specifically Ricoeurian or a more general one, environmental hermeneutics has as its chief aim to not remain in theory but to impact practices. All practice—all action—is interpretation. In order to achieve this kind of impact, environmental hermeneutics, Ricoeurian and otherwise, must engage other environmental sciences and disciplines and that engagement must be reciprocated. I chose to begin this inquiry with environmental identity because I believe it to be fundamental. However we choose to act in terms of the health of the planet will be determined by who we choose to be. Beyond the cogito *that* we are is the question of *who* we are. Beyond the will to survive (again, *that* we are), we must ask ourselves *how* we are to be. The answer to the question "who?" is also the answer to the question "how?." As Ricoeur said, if there is to be humanity after us, there must be nature after us. But who are we? Environmental identity must be carnal. It must be formed by *touching* the earth if there is to be a nature after us that will allow human life to remain.

NOTES

1. Paul Ricoeur, *Oneself as Another*, translated by Kathleen Blamey (Chicago: University of Chicago Press, 1992).

2. See David Utsler, "Paul Ricoeur's Hermeneutics as a Model for Environmental Philosophy," in *Philosophy Today* 53, no. 2 (Summer 2009): 173–78; David Utsler, "Who Am I, Who Are These People, and What Is the Place? A Hermeneutic Account of Self, Others, and Environments," in *Placing Nature on the Borders of Religion, Philosophy and Ethics*, edited buy Forrest Clingerman and Mark Dixon (Burlington: Ashgate Publishing, 2001), 139–51; David Utsler, "Environmental Hermeneutics and Environmental/Eco-Psychology: Explorations in Environmental Identity," in *Interpreting Nature: The Emerging Field of Environmental Hermeneutics*, edited by Forrest Clingerman, Brian Treanor, Martin Drenthen, and David Utsler (New York: Fordham University Press, 2014), 123–40.

3. Ricoeur, *Oneself as Another*, 1.

4. Ricoeur, *Oneself as Another*, 317.

5. Ricoeur, *Oneself as Another*, 311.

6. Ricoeur, *Oneself as Another*, 297.

7. Friedrich Wilhelm Nietzsche, *The Gay Science: Or, the Joyful Wisdom* (Whithorn: Anodos Books, 2019), 88.

8. Ricoeur, *Oneself as Another*, 143.

9. Ricoeur, *Oneself as Another*, 18.

10. Ricoeur, *Oneself as Another*, 2.

11. Ricoeur, *Oneself as Another*, 8.

12. Ricoeur, *Oneself as Another*, 297.

13. Richard Kearney, "Between Flesh and Text: Ricoeur's Carnal Hermeneutics," in *Eco-ethica* 5 (2016): 219–31. For another account of this trajectory of Ricoeur's thought, see Richard Kearney's chapter, "The Recovery of the Flesh in Ricoeur and Merleau-Ponty," in *Somatic Desire: Recovering Corporeality in Contemporary Thought*, edited by Sarah Horton, Stephen Mendelsohn, Christine Rojcewicz, and Richard Kearney (Lanham, MD: Lexington Books, 2019), 41–55. See especially pages 48–52.

14. Paul Ricoeur, *Freedom and Nature: The Voluntary and the Involuntary*, translated by Erazim V. Kohák (Evanston, IL: Northwestern University Press, 1966).

15. Richard Kearney, *Touch: Recovering Our Most Vital Sense* (New York: Columbia University Press, 2021), 93.

16. Richard Louv, *Last Child in the Woods* (Chapel Hill, NC: Algonquin Books of Chapel Hill, 2008), 55.

17. Ricoeur, *Oneself as Another*, 318. Emphasis original.

18. Ricoeur, *Oneself as Another*, 322.

19. Ricoeur, *Oneself as Another*, 317.

20. I am using the term "earth-nature" to denote the part of nature specifically in question for the purposes of this chapter and the book as a whole. In the first chapter, I briefly touched upon the problems with the term "nature" and that, in one sense, there is no such thing as nature at all, other than, perhaps, to say as Pesoa's poem did that it is "parts without a whole." But while environmental identity can be spoken of in many ways, my focus here is narrowly on that nature upon which we depend for life in ways that are primordially necessary.

21. Steven Vogel, *Thinking Like a Mall: Environmental Philosophy After the End of Nature* (Cambridge, MA: MIT Press, 2016). See chapter 6, "The Silence of Nature."

22. Cf. Richard Kearney, *On Stories* (New York: Routledge, 2002).

23. Donatella Ester Di Cesare, *Utopia of Understanding: Between Babel and Auschwitz*, translated by Niall Keane (Albany: SUNY Press, 2012). See especially chapter 4, "Exiled in Language."

24. Paul Ricoeur, *On Translation*, translated by Eileen Brennan with an Introduction by Richard Kearney (New York: Routledge, 2006), 23.

25. Hans-Georg Gadamer, *Truth and Method*, Second, Revised Edition, translation revised by Joel Weinsheimer and Donald G. Marshall (New York: Continuum, 1989 [2004]), 470.

26. Richard Kearney and Melissa Fitzpatrick, *Radical Hospitality: From Thought to Action* (New York: Fordham University Press, 2021), 110.

27. Hans-Georg Gadamer, *Philosophical Hermeneutics*, translated and edited by David E. Linge (Berkeley: University of California Press, 1976), 31.

28. Gadamer, *Philosophical Hermeneutics*, 103. Emphasis mine.

29. I have not drawn upon the work of David Abram, especially his *Spell of the Sensuous*, or the work of Merleau-Ponty upon which much of Abram's work draws. To do so is beyond the scope of the present work, but certainly would aid in addressing the questions concerning language and intersubjectivity.

30. The discussion of intersubjectivity with other beings also raises the question of mutual recognition. First, not all other-than-human beings are the same. One cannot homogenize "nature" and speak of intersubjectivity or mutual recognition with a tree, for instance, the same way one might speak of it with one's cat. The ideas of intersubjectivity and mutual recognition can only be analyzed and evaluated in particular cases with different species of beings.

31. Ricoeur, *Oneself as Another*, 324.

32. Paul Ricoeur, *Time and Narrative, Vol. 3*, translated by Kathleen Blamey and David Pellauer (Chicago: University of Chicago Press, 1988), 231.

33. Kearney, *Touch*, 117.

34. See the excellent collection of essays in *Anacarnation and Returning to the Lived Body with Richard Kearney*, edited by Brian Treanor and James L. Taylor (New York: Routledge, 2023). See, especially, chapter 3, "The Embodied Human Being in Touch with the World: Richard Kearney, and Hedwig Conrad-Martius in Conversation" by Christina M. Gschwandtner. See, also, *Somatic Desire* referenced in footnote 13.

35. Paul Ricoeur, *The Conflict of Interpretations*, edited by Don Ihde (Evanston, IL: Northwestern University Press, 1974), 16.

36. Gadamer, *Philosophical Hermeneutics* 15.

37. Ricoeur, *The Conflict of Interpretations*, 17.

38. Angela J. Hanscom, *Balanced and Barefoot: How Unrestricted Outdoor Play Makes for Strong, Confident, and Capable Children* (Oakland: New Harbinger Publications, Inc., 2016), 45.

39. Richard Louv, *The Nature Principle: Reconnecting with Life in a Virtual Age* (Chapel Hill, NC: Algonquin Books of Chapel Hill, 2012), 3.

40. Ricoeur, *The Conflict of Interpretations*, 16–17.

41. I remain indebted to, and challenged by, Brian Treanor of Loyola Marymount University in Los Angeles for our many conversations over the years on the problematic nature of the "metaphor of the text" for interpretation generally. Chapter 6 will explore this topic further.

42. Paul Ricoeur, *From Text to Action: Essays in Hermeneutics, II*, translated by Kathleen Blamey and John B. Thompson (Evanston, IL: Northwestern University Press, 1991), 87. Emphasis original.

Chapter 3

Anthropocentrism vs. Non-Anthropocentrism

A Hermeneutic Alternative

A central question in environmental philosophy from its beginnings has been the problem of anthropocentrism and its harmful consequences for the environment; the response to this problem has come in the various forms of non-anthropocentrism that argue for alternative ways to understand the human relationship to the other-than-human world. In this chapter, I argue that approaching the human relationship to the environment by seeking to determine the correct "center" from which to reason is fundamentally limited and not sufficient to address the ecological crisis we currently face. Furthermore, the reduction of the problem to such an either/or proposition cannot account for the multiple stakeholders (human and otherwise) and their legitimate concerns to survive and to live well. I then propose a hermeneutic alternative, a specifically Ricoeurian alternative. I further argue that we must take a more multicentric or "polycentric" approach that recognizes legitimate claims and concerns that cannot be satisfied from a traditional singularly centric ethic. Legitimate claims and concerns from various "centers" call for adjudication and practical wisdom. Ricoeur's mediating style of hermeneutics provides just such a pathway toward adjudication.

ANTHROPOCENTRISM

Terms, first and foremost, must be defined. What is anthropocentrism in the mind of its critics? A short answer is that humans alone have moral standing and value, and that "moral obligations extend only to other humans."[1] The consequence of this view is that since other beings do not have moral standing, how we make use of them is not a moral concern. It is hard to imagine that there are any truly thoughtful people in these times who would defend this understanding of anthropocentrism as justifiable. Many defenders of anthropocentrism point out that what non-anthropocentrists are really object-ing to is human chauvinism and speciesism.[2] Environmental pragmatist Bryan Norton has argued that anthropocentrism is only problematic in its "strong" form that fails to rationally question the way in which humans fulfill desires and needs. "Strong anthropocentrism" has no mechanism to distinguish between destructive versus nondestructive satisfactions of desires and needs. He proposes a "weak anthropocentrism" that uses rational means to satisfy a desire or need, thus allowing for the satisfaction of human desires and needs but that do so in environmentally friendly ways. Thus, weak anthropocen-trism places a limit on human behavior and "provides a basis for criticisms of value systems which are purely exploitative of nature."[3]

The defenders of anthropocentrism simply wish to say that human con-cerns and needs are legitimate and that it is perfectly reasonable to look after our own interests. Anthropocentrism need not be "strong" or chauvinistic and can include the preservation of the environment. Wilfred Beckerman and Joanna Pasek point out that no other species in the environment takes into consideration the intrinsic value of other species. This is a particularly human reflective activity. As such, citing Bernard Williams, Beckerman and Pasek argue that concern for the environment expresses culture, not nature.[4] As Ricoeur said in "Ethics, Politics, Ecology," which was discussed at length in chapter 1, "the preservation of nature is a part of the humanist project"[5] due to the fact that since we are the most ill-equipped of all species to survive, survival becomes a cultural project.[6]

NON-ANTHROPOCENTRISM

But, the non-anthropocentrist might inquire, if anthropocentrism can include nonhuman life, is it not equally the case that various non-anthropocentric environmental ethics can just as easily be extended to include human life? In fact, it seems, for example, that biocentrism (a "life-centered" ethic) already includes all forms of life. Ecocentrism, which emphasizes the interconnected-ness between living things, could likewise be understood to already include human life without having to say so. Anthropocentrism, both might object, has to self-consciously and deliberately include nonhuman life, such inclu-sion is not inherent to it. But, may the non-anthropocentrist rightly make this claim?

Charles S. Brown has rightly observed that the egalitarianism of various non-anthropocentrisms has its own set of limitations. While the promise of solidarity with nature is the hope of non-anthropocentrism, the danger lies in that the "radical egalitarianism of ecocentrism will, however, collapse into nihilism if no distinctions of value are made."[7] What Brown suggests instead is that we balance what he calls "benign forms of anthropocentrism" with "benign forms of ecocentrism"[8] (and I think the same applies to any form of non-anthropocentrism). Brown's arguments point to the notion that both anthropocentrism and non-anthropocentrism can be good or bad depending on how they are employed; and that each (in their benign forms) can place a check on each other. If Brown is onto something here, his thoughts suggest that there is no absolute center of moral reasoning in environmental ethics. Rather, there are relative centers of concern that need to be dialectically related to address the interrelated and individual legitimate concerns of each.

The obvious implication here is that the long-running belief of many environmental philosophers that environmental ethics is a matter of locating the correct center from which to reason is mistaken. Lars Samuelsson, in an article titled "At the Centre of What?" argued that the centrism language "is ambiguous, confusing and misleading, and that is a reason for both writers and teachers of environmental ethics to take a critical stance towards it."[9] What might such a critical stance look like? I see at least three parts to such a critical stance: 1) The idea of an absolute center must be given up altogether (while acknowledging and holding on to what the various "centrisms" get right, despite being incomplete). Furthermore, the lack of an absolute center would indicate that the answer to the ecological crisis is not an overarching system (such as bio- or eco-centrism) that can direct human activity, especially in individual and particular cases. Prudential wisdom is necesssary; 2) The recognition that there are particular relative centers that have legitimate claims and all must be taken into consideration; 3) So as to not merely curse the darkness, an alternative must be given that has the capacity to adjudicate between potentially conflicting relative centers. What I will propose is a hermeneutic alternative drawn from the thought of Paul Ricoeur. In what follows, I will address the first three items listed and then outline elements of the particularly Ricoeurian alternative I think his work offers to the conversation.

TIME TO DE-CENTER

As we reflect on the multiple constructions of an environmental ethic in terms of various "centrisms," it becomes apparent that all of them are framed as a more environmentally conscious response to anthropocentrism. Anthropocentrism, taking humans as the center of the moral universe, is at the core of the ecological crisis. Therefore, we must eschew anthropocentrism in favor of another center that will be the right one to "save the environment."

In biocentrism, a reverence for life (bios) is taken to be that center. The center from which we reason morally is the respect for all life because things that are alive wish to stay alive. If we rightly respect this will to life, we will finally recognize that human life does not have the sole claim on moral consider-ability and we will have finally "overcome" anthropocentrism. Ecocentrism, while likewise seeking to overcome anthropocentrism, places systems and relations at the center of moral reasoning. All life is interconnected, so we must recognize that interconnectedness and build our environmental ethic based on that.

What if the response to a perceived environmentally destructive anthropo-centrism is not simply to locate a new center? From the problems associated with anthropocentrism it does not follow that the answer lies in exchanging one center for another. It almost seems as if having a center was assumed and, therefore, a different strategy was never considered. What if the problem of anthropocentrism, in addition to the problem of thinking humans are at the center of moral considerability, is that centrist-oriented thinking itself is the problem and is inadequate in addressing environmental concerns? Perhaps it is time to de-center. It seems a more workable strategy would be to recognize that there is nothing intrinsically wrong with human interests, but to also rec-ognize that the fulfillment of human interests is absolutely contingent upon other centers of concern.

Along this same line, Mary Midgely practically and wisely observed that it is necessary "to recognize that people do right, not wrong, to have a particular regard for their own kin and species. From a practical angle, this recognition does not harm green causes, because the measures needed today to save the human race are, by and large, the same measures that are needed to save the rest of the biosphere."[10] Human interests cannot be separated from the inter-ests of all life (biocentrism) and those of ecosystems (ecocentrism) except at our peril. There is no absolute, overarching center, only smaller relative cen-ters that simultaneously have distinct and interrelated interests. In rejecting an absolute anthropocentrism (which would simply be chauvinism), what is not precluded is a relative anthropocentrism that, as Midgely says, is not wrong.

I would like to interject as relevant here something that I will revisit in chapter 4. Discussions of "saving the environment" are already anthropo-centric in this more modest, relative way. As Ricoeur said, it is we humans who are raising these questions.[11] And, I would add, we are raising them in our own interest of survival. Should human life meet its own extinction, such questions will not matter and will no longer be asked. And, if we are no lon-ger here, the planet will restore itself in time. So, when we ask, for example, whether we should recognize the intrinsic value of other-than-human nature, we are asking for ourselves in the interest of our own survival.

The time has come to de-center environmental ethics. But to de-center environmental ethics does not imply making it a-centric. Anthony Weston expressed this same point two decades ago when he wrote: "A decentered world is not (need not be) an a-centered world. Instead, we envision a many-centered world, a diversity of centers, a world of thick and polynodal texture."[12] Weston's "multicentric" argument seeks not to reject one centrism in favor of another, but aims at de-centering. In rejecting any "monocentrism,"[13] Weston insists that this does not imply that there are no centers (a-centric) but that the recognition of many centers is required, none of which is necessarily privileged over the others. In response to biocentrists and ecocentrists who would argue that they are already in some sense multicentric and include humankind as well, Weston responds thusly:

> Multicentrism also suggests an unexpected critical angle on familiar mega-centrisms such as biocentrism and ecocentrism. It begins to seem that these views are emboldened to call themselves centrisms in the first place only because they are—implicitly—wholly oppositionally defined. The aim is to center on something bigger than humanity. . . . I suspect, then, that such megacentrisms really represent only a form of resistance or refusal of the usual anthropocentrism.[14]

Both biocentrism and ecocentrism (and other such centrisms) are conceived in opposition to anthropocentrism. All such views are constructed on the presupposition that there is an overarching center from which to reason. Multicentrism (or polycentrism) is not a "meta-centrism" but the recognition that there are numerous relative centers, none of which are a center that any of the others orbit around. Rather, there are interactions and interconnections between them all. Multicentrism, unfortunately, since the time Weston proposed it some twenty years ago, has not gained much traction. Most of the discourse in environmental ethics today still "centers" around avoiding anthropocentrism in favor of adopting some other center of moral reasoning. Before turning finally to the hermeneutic alternative (that I hope will provide some strength to multicentrism), I move to my second claim that we must recognize relative centers and their legitimate claims. The idea of relative centers flows directly from the idea of multicentrism and will flow into what I will explain as a hermeneutic alternative to the oppositional nature of the discourse on anthropocentrism/non-anthropocentrism.

RELATIVE CENTERS AND
HERMENEUTIC ADJUDICATION

The first thing to address here is that relative centers do not imply relativistic centers. It would be a mistake that the rejection of an absolute center from which to reason morally about environmental concerns implies relativism. More aptly considered, the reality of multiple centers must raise the question of how these many centers of concern relate to one another. In agreement with Weston, I maintain that to de-center does not imply a-centering. To understand relative centers, a clarification as to what a "center" is would be helpful. Here I think of Aristotle in Physics, where he referred to the relativity of directions in space.[15] Directions such as up and down, right or left only make sense relative to the placement of a body. What we refer to as a center, then, is a body in place that, relative to it, has an up, down, front, back, right and left. For, as Aristotle said in that same passage in Physics, the absence of a body in place is a void.[16] From this, it becomes apparent that in some sense, for we as humans to refer to "the environment" is already hopelessly anthropocentric. For to have an environment, that which "environs" me, I must stand at the center of it. What is understood to be "around" me in all directions is determined and defined relative to my position. Of course, this physical center is not equivalent to a moral center but, by analogy we can grasp that humans as a relative center of moral concern cannot claim to be an absolute center of moral concern. We must recognize that there are other beings with legitimate claims to their own moral concern relative to our own.

Of course, what we refer to as the environment (which is "our" environment) is comprised of countless particulars all of which are placed centrally to every direction that surrounds ("environs") each one of them. To speak of an environment in its physical sense necessarily refers to individual bodies in place. We might also speak of these various "centers" conceptually. Just as "anthropocentrism" does not necessarily refer to to the distinct physical center of each and every individual human being, but to the moral centrality of the species, we can also consider the moral centrism of multiple kinds of beings—indeed, of every existing species. For the purposes of a Ricoeurian environmental hermeneutics, I will assume the moral sense primarily that, in different contexts and with different species, may also include individual members of the species.[17]

HERMENEUTIC POLYCENTRISM AND
THE SURPLUS OF MEANING

What the various approaches to and debates about the various "centrisms" represent is fundamentally a conflict of interpretations. The basic question of environmental ethics asks what the relationship of human beings to the other-than-human world is, or rather, what it should be. How should we orient ourselves to the world in the interest of environmental sustainability? Where is the locus of moral concern? What sorts of beings have moral considerability? So, to insist, for example, that we should take a particular non-anthropocentric position is an ethical position about our orientation to the world. It is an interpretation. Moreover, it is an interpretation that claims it is the correct one and other interpretations are incorrect. Such an either/or approach works for many things that are unambiguous, but either/or binary answer to many ethical questions are inadequate. This is where a "hermeneutical orientation" is needful for environmental ethics.

Ricoeur says that "there is interpretation wherever there is multiple meaning, and it is in interpretation that the plurality of meaning is made manifest."[18] The presence of multiple meanings can seem nowhere more obvious than in the interplay between complex ecosystems, global climate change, human needs and endeavors, and the whole of environmental issues. Hence, the need for environmental hermeneutics, likewise, would seem obvious. Should we be ecocentric or biocentric? Should we be weakly anthropocentric or strongly anthropocentric? Such questions cannot capture or encompass the multiple meanings and level of meanings in the contemporary environmental landscape.

Similarly, Ricoeur addressed himself to the debate between Hans-Georg Gadamer and Jürgen Habermas regarding the hermeneutics of tradition and the critique of ideology. Ricoeur said the stakes of the debate presented and alternative. What is needed? Is it "a hermeneutical consciousness or a critical consciousness"?[19] Ricoeur, instead, said that the alternative itself needed to be challenged. He asks: "Is it possible to formulate a hermeneutics that would render justice to the critique of ideology, that would show the necessity of the latter at the very heart of its own concerns."[20] What Ricoeur wants to show is that hermeneutics can include what critique demands and that the critique of ideology presupposes hermeneutics. Hermeneutics is critique and critique is inherently hermeneutical.[21]

Yet, Ricoeur does not merely want to do some form of Hegelian synthesis between the two: "My aim is not to fuse the hermeneutics of tradition and the critique of ideology in a super-system that would encompass both. As I said at the outset, each speaks from a different place. Nonetheless, each may be

asked to recognize the other, not as a position that is foreign and purely hostile, but as one that raises in its own way a legitimate claim."[22] This is a perfect
instance of how Richard Kearney describes Ricoeur's philosophical attitude.
In his introduction to Ricoeur's *On Translation*, Kearney writes: "Ricoeur
was an inveterate mediator, someone who navigated and negotiated transits
between rival intellectual positions. He was unequalled as a diplomat of
philosophical exchange, forever finding a point of commerce—if not always
resolution—between ostensibly irreconcilable viewpoints."[23] This approach
of Ricoeur's hermeneutics, one of mediation and negotiation, should be the
defining characteristic of the polycentric approach to the divide between
anthropocentrism and non-anthropocentrism.

The way in which this problem has been addressed traditionally in environmental ethics can be described as hostile. Hostility, that is, between human
concerns and the concerns of nonhuman others. One side of the binary is
foreign to the other and marked by the lack of recognition. However, a
de-centered, polycentric approach, hermeneutically framed, would insist that
each "center" has a legitimate claim, and that these claims can be mutually
recognized as speaking from their own place. The hostility is a kind of hermeneutical distanciation in which there is an alienation between the human
concerns and the concerns of the other-than-human. Many approaches that
oppose themselves to anthropocentrism subconsciously reject the notion of
distanciation, tending more to homogenize difference. Environmental consciousness, conceived hermeneutically, does not wish to reject distanciation
but instead to recognize that it is from the place of distance that each "center"
is allowed to speak from its own place. The interrelation between beings,
ecologically, is predicated on maintaining nonhostile distance as a sort of
hermeneutical tension between distanciation and belonging.

In the context of historical consciousness, Ricoeur maintains that there is a
sort of "general opposition between belonging and alienating distanciation."
He writes: "There is thus a paradox of otherness, a tension between proximity
and distance, which is essential to historical consciousness."[24] Ricoeur then
likens this to Gadamer's concept of the "fusion of horizons." Ricoeur says of
Gadamer: "This concept signifies that we live neither in closed horizons, nor
within one unique horizon. Insofar as the fusion of horizons excludes the idea
of total and unique knowledge, this concept implies a tension between what
is one's own and what is alien, between the near and the far; and hence the
play of difference is included in the process of convergence."[25] I argue that
this same tension applies to environmental consciousness.

An exclusive emphasis on either we are different from nature (anthropocentrism) or one with nature (eco/bio-centrism) excludes both difference
and the process of convergence. However, the point of a hermeneutical
polycentrism is to maintain this tension and the play between the poles to the

end of constructing an environmental ethic built upon hospitality rather than hostility. Human exceptionalism must be balanced and held in tension with being a "fragment of the ecosystem." So, what is true of historical consciousness bears a resemblance to what is true of environmental consciousness. There is a sense in which we must fuse our own horizons with that of the other-than-human world if we are to find practical solutions for the environmental crisis.

THE CONFLICT OF INTERPRETATIONS
AND PRACTICAL WISDOM

One question immediately arises from the prospect of a hermeneutical polycentric approach where each "center" can be understood to raise legitimate claims, speaking from its own place. That is, what of conflicting environmental interpretations? What happens when one legitimate claim excludes that of the other or raises seemingly insurmountable conflicts between the two? It is easy enough when certain conflicting interpretations (through a critical environmental consciousness) can be identified as unacceptable interpretations. But that does not exclude the cases where legitimate needs and concerns can be found to conflict.

There are seemingly innumerable ways these conflicts can be conceived. Just between human beings alone there may be conflicts of interpretation involving how land should be used or developed. What about conflicts of interpretation, for example, between local communities and their environmental identities connected to place with the economic need of tourist revenue? Then there are conflicts between human beings and biodiversity, jobs versus forest preservation, and so on. This section also, for the sake of argument, assumes that these are conflicts between legitimate needs and concerns, not a case, for example, of a factory that needs to dispose of chemical waste and wants to do so by dumping it in a river, thereby poisoning the wildlife and a source of income and nutrition for indigenous peoples. Conflicting interpretations between legitimate needs and concerns cannot always be easily adjudicated. Practical wisdom, phronesis, is needed. Brian Treanor provides this apt definition of practical wisdom:

> Phronesis comes into its own in the messy situation of ethical ambiguity. The person with practical wisdom is able to judge well with respect to choices in particular circumstances that do not fall neatly under general rules for conduct, either when the particular situation seems to merit an exception to the universal rule or when two ethical guidelines or rules come into conflict.[26]

Paul Ricoeur speaks of "conflictual situations" in which practical wisdom must return "to the initial intuition of ethics . . . that is, to the vision or aim of the 'good life' with and for others in just institutions."[27] What Ricoeur's statement here reveals is that when there is no clear rule or obligation, we have to ask what would be best, that is, best for a good life with others and for others, embodied in institutions that are just. Our decisions suggest that our concern is simply to envision what sort of world it is in which we, together, wish to live. Ricoeur's connecting of the ethical aim with practical wisdom further strengthens the notion of polycentrism. He recognizes that conflicting interpretations arise from plurality and are, therefore, political. Environmental conflicts (whether between persons or groups of persons or that of human claims and concerns with those of the other-than-human world) are also political conflicts where decisions affect the parties involved. In his discussion of practical wisdom in Oneself as Another, Ricoeur says that it is conflict that drives us to a "court of appeal" manifested in the three areas of "the universal self, the plurality of persons, and the institutional environment."[28] So, rather than seeking to find the correct "center" to govern our decisions, Ricoeur's conception of the operation of practical wisdom calls for individual and collective centers to raise their claim.

DELIBERATIVE POLYCENTRISM

As such, polycentrism is also deliberative. Ricoeur asks how it is that moral philosophy appeals to the idea of deliberating well. Ricoeur places this discussion in the context of the tragic and notes that tragedy, "having disoriented the gaze, condemns the person of praxis to reorient action, at his or her own risk, in the sense of a practical wisdom in situation that best responds to tragic wisdom."[29] Is there any clearer case of the tragic than that of our contemporary environmental crisis in its systemic and political roots? Is there any clearer case in our time than the environmental crisis that demands the response of practical wisdom to tragic wisdom? And, is there any clearer case than the environmental crisis that demands a deliberative rationality from the grassroots and at the institutional level?

Anthony Weston rightly points out: "We cannot practice ethics on our own. Once other centers are acknowledged, always somewhat opaque to us as we are to them, there is no alternative but to work things out together, as far as possible, when all are affected by the decisions taken."[30] Polycentrism (or "multicentrism" in Weston's terminology) recognizes the importance of deliberation because it recognizes there are many stakeholders in the environment, human and other-than-human alike. Weston sees this as well: "Multicentrism's most striking implication is its move toward a 'communicative ethics' that ranges far beyond the human sphere. Imperative is to move from the familiar one-species monologue to a truly multipolar dialogue."[31] Drawing on a variety of sources from ancient native wisdom to discoveries in recent science, Weston points out that we are always interacting with all aspects of our environment, we are always interacting with other "centers," and negotiating those relationships.

A result of taking a polycentric position is what R. Bruce Hall refers to as "pluralizing nature." That is, nature is not one monolithic thing but is made up of multiple beings and, therefore, requires openness and listening. "Pluralizing nature facilitates the collaboration and deliberation that resolves environmental conflict and implements solutions. . . . Resolving environmental conflicts requires collaborative, deliberative efforts where participants comprehend and respect one another's perspectives. . . . Pluralizing nature increases the decision space."[32] Hull's perspective on "pluralizing nature" strikes me as deeply hermeneutical, for it recognizing that there is at once multiple meaning and various layers of meaning inscribed into the environment. Monolithic approaches that seek to find the sole, correct center fail to account for the character of polysemy, which not only characterizes language, as Ricoeur has it, but also the environment itself.

CONCLUSION

A hermeneutical approach to the debate between anthropocentrism and non-anthropocentrism frees us from having to reduce environmental ethics to a single center that would simply a complex problem and from having to choose between "centers." Instead, a Ricoeurian environmental hermeneutics recognizes that each should be allowed to speak from its own place and raise legitimate claims and that different centers must be held in a hermeneutical tension between distanciation and belonging. A Ricoeurian environmental hermeneutics also recognizes the inevitability of the conflict of (even legitimate) interpretations, which would then open up the space for dialogue and adjudication following the guidance of practical wisdom.

Environmental hermeneutics suggests that the long debate over the various monocentrisms has been largely misguided. This, of course, is a bold claim that likewise suggests that a great deal of writing over the last several decades in environmental ethics has missed the point. But in a highly complex world with an increasing diversity of the sources of our environmental problems, it is time to abandon this monocentric sort of reasoning. The crisis we face and even the threat of our own extinction cannot be solved simply by being non-anthropocentric. We must adopt a multicentric "communicational ethics" that includes what Ricoeur calls an "ethics of belonging," to this end: "The subtlety of this fragile equilibrium must be maintained, at once within nature [and all its parts] and as the exception to nature."[33]

NOTES

1. *Environmental Ethics: The Big Questions*, edited by David R. Keller (Chichester, UK: Wiley-Blackwell, 2010), 10.

2. Cf. Tim Hayward, "Anthropocentrism: A Misunderstood Problem," *Environmental Values* 6, no. 1 (1997): 49–63.

3. Bryan G. Norton, "Environmental Ethics and Weak Anthropocentrism," *Environmental Ethics* 6, no. 2 (1984): 135.

4. Wilfred Beckerman and Joanna Pasek, "In Defense of Anthropocentrism," in *Environmental Ethics: The Big Questions*, 83–88. I am citing the anthologized version of this essay. It originally appeared in Wilfred Beckerman and Joana Pasek, *Justice, Posterity, and the Environment* (Oxford: Oxford University Press, 2001), 129–35.

5. Paul Ricoeur, "Ethics, Politics, Ecology" in *Philosophy, Ethics, & Politics*, translated by Kathleen Blamey (Cambridge, UK: Polity Press, 2020), 114.

6. See, Ricoeur, "Ethics, Politics, Ecology," 104.

7. Charles S. Brown, "Anthropocentrism and Ecocentrism: The Quest for a New Worldview," *The Midwest Quarterly* 36, no. 2 (1995): 191–202.

8. Brown, 201.

9. Lars Samuelsson, "At the Centre of What?" in *Environmental Values* 22, no. 25 (October 2013): 643.

10. Mary Midgley, "The End of Anthropocentrism," in *Environmental Ethics: The Big Questions*, 142. I am citing the anthologized version of this essay. It originally appeared in *Philosophy and the Natural Environment*, edited by Robin Attfield and Andrew Belsey, Royal Institute of Philosophy Supplement 36 (Cambridge, UK: Cambridge University Press, 1994), 103–12.

11. Paul Ricoeur, "Ethics, Politics, Ecology, 113.

12. Anthony Weston, "Multicentrism: A Manifesto," *Environmental Ethics* 26, no. 1 (2004): 30. This article was later published in Weston's book *The Incompleat Eco-Philosopher: Essays from the Edges of Environmental Ethics* (Albany: SUNY Press, 2009).

13. Weston, *The Incompleat Eco-Philosopher*, 93.

14. Weston, 98–99.

15. See Aristotle, *Physics*, Book IV, Ch. 1, 208b, 15–19.

16. Aristotle, *Physics*, Book IV, Ch. 1, 208b, 25.

17. For the purposes of this chapter, I am speaking more generally. A different and more focused discussion, outside of the scope of this chapter, would be concerning making distinctions in kinds of species where each particular member of that species has a claim to individual moral concern vs. those where it is understood the species itself and not its individual members. For example, for a livable environment for humans, we understand that trees are necessary; but we also understand that cutting

down individual trees is not a moral violation. Human beings, by contrast, have a center of moral concern as a species, but also each individual human is also its own moral center.

18. Paul Ricoeur, *The Conflict of Interpretations*, edited by Don Ihde (Evanston, IL: Northwestern University Press, 1974), 13.

19. Paul Ricoeur, *From Text to Action: Essays in Hermeneutics II*, translated by Kathleen Blamey and John B. Thompson (Evanston, IL: Northwestern University Press, 1991), 270.

20. Ricoeur, *From Text to Action*, 270.

21. Gadamer argued that the hermeneutics of tradition was not merely passing down tradition unreflectively, but that the "historical life of a tradition depends on being constant assimilated and interpreted" (see *Truth and Method*, 398). For Gadamer, hermeneutics has critique built into it. But also, concerning Habermas, Gadamer wrote: "Habermas sees the critique of ideology as the means of unmasking the 'deceptions of language.' But this critique, of course, is in itself a linguistic act of reflection" (see Gadamer's *Philosophical Hermeneutics*, 30). In other words, Gadamer himself already recognizes what Ricoeur is aiming at, namely that hermeneutics is critical and critique is hermeneutical.

22. Ricoeur, *From Text to Action*, 294–95.

23. Richard Kearney, "Introduction: Ricoeur's philosophy of translation," in Paul Ricoeur, *On Translation*, translated by Eileen Brennan (New York: Routledge, 2006), vii.

24. Paul Ricoeur, *Hermeneutics and the Human Sciences: Essays on Language, Action, and Interpretation*, edited and translated by John B. Thompson (New York: Cambridge University Press, 1981), 61.

25. Ricoeur, *Hermeneutics and the Human Sciences*, 62.

26. Brian Treanor, *Emplotting Virtue: A Narrative Approach to Environmental Virtue Ethics* (Albany: SUNY Press, 2014), 33. Emphasis original.

27. Paul Ricoeur, *Oneself as Another*, translated by Kathleen Blamey (Chicago: University of Chicago Press, 1992), 240.

28. Ricoeur, *Oneself as Another*, 249–50. Emphasis original.

29. Ricoeur, *Oneself as Another*, 247.

30. Weston, *The Incompleat Eco-Philosopher*, 95. Emphasis original.

31. Weston, *The Incompleat Eco-Philosopher*, 100.

32. R. Bruce Hull, *Infinite Nature* (Chicago: University of Chicago Press, 2006), 5.

33. Ricoeur, "Ethics, Politics, Ecology," 113–14.

Chapter 4

Fragile Earth/Fragile Humanity

Fragility and the Future

What might it mean to refer to the earth as fragile? For the purposes of this chapter, I will define a fragile earth as an earth that is vulnerable to damage. The planet and its ecosystems can be, and have been, gravely damaged. The UN Convention on Biodiversity estimates 18,000–55,000 species go extinct each year, which is approximately 15–150 each day.[1] Ecologists are now watching with a close eye what is referred to as the sixth mass extinction. We are living in a time that has been dubbed the Anthropocene, a term defining the current geological age as one in which the current geologic changes and impact on the planet are driven overwhelmingly by human activity (see chapter 1, note 25). Some have opted for the term "Capitalocene" to indicate that the age is not merely the aggregate activity of all human beings but is structurally related to the driving forces of global capitalism.[2] Anthropogenic changes in the earth's climate affect oceans and soil, altering regions of the earth dramatically. The earth as an exploitable commodity is an earth that is perishable.

Despite, however, the fact that the earth is vulnerable to serious damage from human activity, it is far from irreparable. The joke, as it were, is on us. It turns out that the greater fragility, the greater vulnerability, is human life. The danger to a fragile earth presents an even graver danger to a far more fragile humanity. We may burn the earth, but in doing so consign ourselves to the flames. We will be gone, but the planet is a phoenix that will rise from its own ashes. The earth has time. Billions of years perhaps. Humanity does not have that kind of time.

An underlying premise of this chapter, therefore, is that any talk of environmental protection, sustainability, and so forth is ultimately of human concern. While we can and should recognize the value of nonhuman others and the goodness of the earth for itself, apart from any human valuing of it, that does not alter the fact that these questions are being asked by us and will no longer matter should we cease to exist. Concerns that this may lend itself to a worrisome form of anthropocentrism are misguided. What Ricoeur refers to as human exceptionalism does not justify the exploitation of the planet but is not naively or romantically ignorant of the particularities of human life. As Ricoeur stated, "The capacity to question is, until proven otherwise, our privilege and our curse."[3] We humans exist. We wish to continue to exist. We are beings who question. What questions we ask and, more importantly, the kind of answers we give those questions that shape and guide what we do will determine whether human life will, in fact, continue to exist. In this chapter, I will look at Ricoeur's account of fragility and consider the implications of fragility placed within the scope of our global ecological crisis.

A FRAGILE EARTH

Despite the fact that, as said just above, the earth fully has the capacity to restore itself and regenerate ecosystems, we must not diminish the reality of the fragility of the planet in terms of the damage that human activity can cause. The malign effect of human activity is no small matter and is, as Ricoeur said, now a global problem. Indeed, it can be rightly observed that the scale is even beyond the global if we consider the gravest threat to the planet is climate change. Our most serious effect on the planet is caused by our effect upon that which is beyond the planet, and upon which the planet depends, its atmosphere.

Here, I must insert a disclaimer. By the language of "human activity," I do not refer to the aggregate effect of the activity of each individual human as if the solution to our ecological crisis is a matter of persuading each individual human to act differently and in an environmentally sustainable manner. The cause of the ecological crisis is not a matter of mere individual activity, and the solution, likewise, is not a matter of changing mere individual activity. I refer to human activity only in the sense that the kinds of activity that do harm to the planet on such a large scale are perpetrated by humankind. This geologic age is now commonly referred to as the Anthropocene, which is to say that the impact on the earth and the climate from human presence is now measurably significant, if not dominate. This is not to say, however, that all humans are equally implicated, and many are not implicated at all. What is crucial to understand is that these deleterious effects are matters of systems and structures devised by humans. The ecological crisis is a systemic crisis, not a matter of individual responsibility. It is not as if the solution to the ecological crisis is for everyone to start recycling more, buying only "green" products, and stop using plastic straws. The real problem is systemic and rooted in a global paradigm of endless growth. Ian Angus sums it up:

In article after article, book after book, scientists and environmentalists have exposed the devastating effects of constant economic expansion on the global environment. The drive to produce ever more "stuff" is filling our rivers with poison and our air with climate-changing gases. The oceans are dying, species are disappearing at unprecedented rates, water is running short, and soil is eroding much faster than it can be replaced.[4]

But, it seems, that endless growth is sacrosanct and incontestable. We are not to ask about changing systems or structures. Rather, it is within these structures that we can find the solutions to our problems, we are told. As Mark Fisher rightly observed: "The fantasy being that western consumerism, far from being *intrinsically implicated* in systemic global inequalities [and, I would add, ecological destruction], could itself solve them. All we have to do is buy the right products."[5] What this is all indicative of is that the responsibility for the ecological crisis is shifted to the individual and the choices the individual makes rather than where it belongs, the insatiable not-to-be-questioned orthodoxy of unfettered capitalist growth.

And while we speak of climate change, other factors threaten to make the planet uninhabitable by humans. John Bellamy Foster writes:

Recently, leading scientists . . . have proposed nine planetary boundaries which mark a safe operating space for the planet. Three of these boundaries—climate change, biodiversity, and the nitrogen cycle—have already been crossed, while others, such as freshwater use and ocean acidification, are emerging planetary rifts. In ecological terms, the economy has now grown to a scale and intrusiveness that is both overshooting planetary boundaries and tearing apart the biogeochemical cycles of the planet.[6]

So, yes, the earth is fragile and is under threat of such grave damage that its systems will not be able to function to maintain a healthy planet. Certainly not in an absolute sense, but to a small extent the planet is dependent upon humankind to restrain our actions such to prevent the kinds of global damage of which we are capable. However, the stark reality is that the planet is not dependent upon human life in any way whatsoever to *be*, to exist. Any harm caused by human action will not threaten the planet's existence. The same cannot be said about human existence. Our existence is entirely dependent upon the planet and its systems such that if we destroy their necessary functioning, we condemn ourselves. Human fragility is of an entirely different kind, not merely degree.

ASYMMETRICAL DEPENDENCE:
THE ROOT OF HUMAN FRAGILITY

In the opening sentence in the Preface to his excellent and thought-provoking book *A World Not Made for Us*, Keith R. Peterson writes: "This book attempts to define the core principle that should inform collective thinking about the global ecological crisis, namely, the recognition of human asymmetrical dependence upon the more-than-human world."[7] Peterson points out a glaringly obvious fact, yet one that has been given little systematic philosophical attention within the literature of environmental philosophy and ethics. We are utterly, absolutely, and necessarily dependent upon the more-than-human world, and that world is not dependent in the least upon us. "Asymmetrical" is a rather kind and generous characterization. A one-sided, nonreciprocal dependence is more to the point. We need the more-than-human world for our existence, but the earth would continue to turn without the briefest pause if the last member of humankind passed. We simply cannot reciprocate what the more-than-human world provides for human life. The best we can do—and ought to do—is to cease to do harm.

The acknowledgment of this condition is imperative if we are to assume the responsibility that Ricoeur and Jonas describe, a responsibility that is the "object of an ethics." Our asymmetrical dependence becomes the ground on which we imagine a world that can unfold before us that will make the continued existence of humankind possible, and more than merely possible, but in a way in which humankind may continue to thrive and flourish. Such an imagined world can take many shapes and forms, but whatever that world might turn out to be, it will need to be one of genuine sustainability, equity, and justice. The recognition of asymmetrical dependence as the root of human fragility is a requirement for the human species to continue to exist in future generations. The failure to come to terms with human fragility in this asymmetric dependence upon the more-than-human world, by contrast, will be the precise cause of our extinction.

The same is true of any individual species. Countless species have become extinct. Scientists tell us there have been five mass extinctions and that we are facing a sixth in our time. Extinction of individual species whether as the regular course of events of mass extinctions or as a consequence of human activity, one thing holds to be true. Not a single disappearance of any species threatens the disappearance of the planet. But no species can live without the earth to sustain them. So, in one sense what Peterson is saying about human asymmetric dependence on the planet is not necessarily unique to our species. Two things, however, are unique to our species: the first is that unlike any other species, we have the capacity in our action and conduct to render the planet uninhabitable. There is no other species on earth whose collective action has perpetrated the extent of damage to the planet as humankind. The second uniqueness is that, as far as we know, we are the only species that, as Ricoeur said, questions, reflects, ponders, and wonders. This simply means that we bear a responsibility that no other species does for our thoughts, words, and actions.

Ricoeur said, referring back to the 1993 interview, "Ethics, Politics, Ecology," that was the subject matter of the first chapter, that for there to be humanity after us, there must be nature after us (see chapter 1, note 38). This statement perfectly captures the notion of asymmetrical dependence. It cannot be turned around to say that for there to be other-than-human nature after us, there must be humanity after us. Other-than-human nature simply does not depend in the least on our continued existence, but we depend upon it utterly. Hence, our questioning, our reflecting, and our acting must invariably give recognition to this fact. So, before inquiring into Ricoeur's account of fragility as necessary for environmental philosophy, I will turn again briefly to Peterson.

In reenvisioning environmental philosophy and ethics, Peterson insists on a critical environmental philosophy that "must first acknowledge that we occupy a world not made for us," which he insists that the "point is to acknowledge that we do not constitute it [more-than-human nature] in many of its most important modes of existence. Our bodies and our minds depend on the more-than-human to provide the content and even forms of thought, while it does not depend on us to be itself."[8] Peterson's observation here certainly lends credence to what was said in chapter 2 concerning environmental identity, namely, that the self is constituted in its relationship to more-than-human nature. As he said, we do not constitute it, but it cannot be reasonably denied that it constitutes us. Our consciousness of ourselves and our understanding of ourselves relies on our environment, and that remains true even if our interpretations of it are faulty.

If we must interpret the world as "not made for us" as Peterson claims, what precisely does this mean? There are two potential understandings of this phrase. The first of which would be to say that the world is not made for us in the sense that we do not belong here. For example, if I am hosting an exclusive event and parties arrive whowere not invited, I must tell them that my event was not made for them. They should not be here. I do not take this to be Peterson's meaning. On what grounds would we exclude humankind from the planet? Such misanthropy lacks philosophical justification. The second, which I do understand Peterson to be saying, is that this world is not made *for us* such that we have any claim to superiority or ownership. For example, if an artisan makes a piece of furniture *for* a family, then what they do with it, how it is decorated, where it is placed, and what it is used for is entirely at the discretion of those for whom it was made. But the world was not made for us in any such way. We are here, that is all. The world is not ours, and there is nothing in human nature that rationally grants us exclusive superiority over it. Peterson's basis for his claim that the world was not made for us lies in the idea of asymmetric dependence. We may claim based on unique human capacities that we are superior to all other existing things, and the world is made for us because of that. The fact remains that we need it, but it does not need us. We have nothing to leverage over the earth, but it leverages its role in our very existence.

Placed in terms of an ethics of hospitality, Richard Kearney and Melissa Fitzpatrick rightly say that the real issue is not us being hospitable to the earth but "that in regard to nature, we are in fact the ones being hosted, which is certainly true," because "human beings are literally constituted by other-than-human others; without other forms of life, we would cease to exist."[9] Whether externally as in the air we breathe, food we consume, and water we drink, or internally as in having the necessary bacteria in our gut, we are utterly and necessarily dependent on that which is *not us*. Oneself truly is another. But what can be said to have any dependence on us in any similar way? Our relationship to the more-than-human world is not remotely reciprocal. Peterson is correct in this, that we must acknowledge our dependence and develop any future environmental philosophy on that reality. With these reflections in mind, I now turn to Ricoeur's account of fragility.

FRAGILITY, RESPONSIBILITY, AND CAPABILITY

Ricoeur introduced the idea of fragility as a way to look at human action in place of the notion of the tragic.[10] The tragic, Ricoeur says, gets used too broadly. A meaning that is closest to the Greek meaning of the tragic refers to "major conflicts in which human beings aggravate the situation and precipitate catastrophe."[11] In place of the tragic, Ricoeur said he preferred to focus on fragility in human action. There are two senses of fragility at work here in Ricoeur's thought. One is the inherent fragility of human action in that (and this is its tie to the tragic), even "the most well-intentioned human actions appear to aggravate the harms they claim to cure."[12] The other is the sense in which something fragile is placed in our care.

The primary purpose that Ricoeur chose to focus on the fragile in place of the tragic is because of the intrinsic tie that fragility has to responsibility. Fragility becomes a call. "We feel that we are solicited, enjoined by the fragile . . . to bring assistance, of course, but more than that, to promote growth, to foster accomplishment and flourishing."[13] So, beyond the tragic nature of human action that often results in aggravating harms to the environment upon which we depend in our own fragility, the fragility of that which is placed in our care calls us to work to help it grow and flourish. In the context of the environment, there is truly the fragility of human action that is the source of planetary destruction that has placed us in a precarious situation. But it is in the recognition that "a situation exists, but should not exist,"[14] that the call comes from the fragile to take responsibility.

To recall from the first chapter, it is because of our own fragility—that is, being ill-equipped to survive in the environment—that we take up measures to ensure our longevity. Yet, it is those very measures that now threaten our hope of surviving. Hence, responsibility becomes the object of ethics. What is apparent is that this responsibility looks both to the past and to the future. This is also the link of fragility and responsibility to capability. Capability refers to our desire to be the author of our own actions and is that which also makes us responsible. As to the past, as the authors of our own actions, we are called to take responsibility for what has been done. That is, "we maintain that we are ready to repair the damage caused by our actions"[15] and to accept the consequences of our actions. As to the future, capability in relation to the fragility of that which is placed on our care places upon us the responsibility for what will be. Ricoeur writes:

> We are now directed toward the future of a being who has to be helped to sur-
> vive, to grow. And this future can be very distant from our present, as in the
> cases Hans Jonas considered, essentially involving threats to the environment,
> to the ecosystem within which the human adventure unfolds. The imperative
> that requires us to act in such a way as to ensure that humanity will continue
> after us, guides us in a direction of a future as vast as the distance effects of our
> technological interventions.[16]

Here I must reiterate what I said earlier that it is not the case that the responsibility for the environment is not the aggregate of individual choices and capability. Talk of being the author of my own action would seem to suggest the responsibility is on the individual. But Ricoeur explicitly ties fragility to the "public exercise of human action,"[17] rather than that of each individual. In other words, the issue at hand is social and political. Indeed, fragility issues the call to responsibility in terms of capability. In terms of the environmental crisis, the individual is not capable of addressing the crisis nor are individuals aggregately. Thus, responsibility is not placed upon those who are not in a position of capability. Responsibility for the environment must be at the level of the *polis*, which is fraught with its own fragility.

FRAGILITY AND THE *POLIS*

Ricoeur speaks of two kinds of fragility, that of civil society and that of political society. Civil society refers to, primarily, all the varying institutions that make up society and which, frequently, come into conflict as they compete over various and scarce goods (goods such as land, services, education, and so forth). It is political society that is of primary interest in terms of responsibility and the environmental crisis. Political society, the *polis*, has to do with the operations of power. Only at the level of political power can the environmental crisis be addressed. There are two aspects of political society that intersect with regard to power. One is what Ricoeur calls "the desire-to-live-together," the horizontal relation, and the "vertical relation of domination/subordination" at play between leaders and the citizenry.[18] It is the horizontal relation, the desire for community, that should inform the vertical relation of political power.

A fragility that marks the horizontal relation lies in the fact that, although it founds political society, the "desire-to-live-together" is frequently only recognized in times of danger. I think of September 11, 2001, and those horrific attacks, especially on the World Trade Center in New York City. There was a period that followed where the majority of Americans stood in solidarity and there was a great spirit of cooperation. Such solidarity soon deteriorated, however. At the time I am writing this, America has sunk to what I would describe as vicious divisions, nothing like I have witnessed in my lifetime. As Ricoeur will argue, this horizontal relation of "the-desire-to-live-together" is necessary to maintain the fruitfulness of the vertical relation of political power. When we fail to share in this desire in solidarity, the breakdown of the *polis* is the consequence.

Ricoeur wrote that, ideally: "We would like to have the horizontal tie of cooperation engender and nourish the vertical tie of domination."[19] But even if the horizontal is fully living in a cooperative bond, the vertical still has its own fragility inherent to it. In terms of representative democracy, it often turns out that political representatives are often motivated by the particulars of their world. For example, here in the United States we know well that politicians are far more motivated by the desires of big donors than the concerns of the average citizen. Many are content to keep citizens immersed in "culture wars" and division as they go about the business of maintaining their power. So, we have on the plane of the horizontal serious divisions with little serious interest in cooperative civil discourse, or what Hannah Arendt simply referred to as "speech," which, when it ends, violence begins.[20] On the plane of the vertical, we have the fragility of political power.

Ricoeur wrote: "The citizen has to know that the great *polis* is fragile, that it rests on a horizontal tie constitutive of the desire-to-live-together; in short, the citizen has to link public salvation to the vitality of community life, where the desire-to-live-together is regenerated."[21] In addition to this, Ricoeur insisted that due to the fragility inherent in the *polis* that intellectuals have a particular responsibility. He said that "it is their job to clarify the confused notions of political rhetoric."[22] As Ricoeur said in "Ethics, Politics Ecology," the role of intellectuals is to be advisors, not to political rulers, but to the people whom they rule.[23] A challenge to this role of the intellectual as advisor to the public is the distrust and rejection of intellectuals and experts. Climate change alone is a great example of how average citizens feel confident that they know better than climate scientists. We live in a time where intellectuals are simply not respected and anti-intellectualism is celebrated.

The role of philosophers as advisors to the public is a complicated one. It should not be understood as merely bringing people around to accepting expert opinion. The real task is to aid the public in how to think about the various issues (such as climate change) with clarity. This is no small challenge. Philosophers should seek to understand the roots of distrust and seek to fulfill the role, much like Ricoeur himself frequently did, of a mediator of conflicts of interpretation. The other challenge philosophers face in this arena is the way language is used in the public sphere since language has such great power to shape perception. For example, scientists and activists are frequently portrayed as "climate alarmists," which suggests that they are overreactors to a problem that does not truly exist. Fostering open and receptive discourse in such an environment faces difficult obstacles.[24]

Thinking of this fragility of the *polis* in terms of the environment and the crisis we face today, we are dwelling within a situation that seems to offer little hope, if any at all. When we think of a perishable earth upon which we, in our own fragility, depend, then a perishing earth means with absolute certainty a perished humanity. What Ricoeur's reflections tie together is that our own perishing and that of the earth is bound together with the perishing of the *polis*. If the *polis* is conceived of as a dialectic of the horizontal desiring to dwell together and the vertical construction of power, the breakdown and death of the *polis* becomes predicated on the breakdown of this dialectic. It strikes me as indisputable that to mitigate the human impact on the planet, institutions on the vertical plane are necessary. Whether on the global level of environmental destruction that is limited to regional impact, institutions are necessary to assemble the necessary resources, mobilize the appropriate groups, and ensure the carrying out of objectives. On the plane of the horizontal, what will be needed is the cooperative spirit that marks the horizontal plane. For that to happen, what is needed is an entire rehabilitation of the role of the intellectual as advisor and a wide acceptance and recognition on the part of the horizontal plane of the importance of the intellectual in public life.

INTERNATIONAL LINGUISTIC AND
NARRATIVE HOSPITALITY

In recognition of the myriad of fragilities that accompany the environmental crisis, what Ricoeur discusses on the international level of the political is needful. In the text from which I have been primarily drawing, Ricoeur is focused on international relations and addressing conflict. His insights, however, have application to the environmental crisis. One of the most crucial things that hermeneutics provides for environmental discourse is the very idea of discourse itself. For hermeneutics, discourse opens up a space between interlocutors where mutual understanding becomes possible. What is required is what Ricoeur refers to as "linguistic hospitality."

The reason linguistic hospitality is necessary for environmental discourse on the international level is because environmental problems are not isolated from other issues. Indeed, economic structures, science and technology, international growth and development, and so forth are all intertwined with environmental problems. This also includes discourses in environmental justice. For instance, Ricoeur states: "So many questions that nourish the general suspicion on the part of third world countries that our problems in the advanced economies are being shifted to them."[25] What is necessary to grasp is that the greatest threats we face in terms of the environment are global and international. Without the cooperation of political leaders on an international level, the prospects of turning the tide of environmental catastrophe seem impossible.

The role of Ricoeur's notion of linguistic hospitality in international political dialogue is of supreme importance. Differing nations and locations, globally, face different regional challenges from the effects of climate change, some far worse than others, as noted, for example, from Ricoeur just above about the shifting of burdens created by advanced economies to Third World countries. In order to begin international cooperation and build international institutions to address these problems, the work of linguistic hospitality must begin. Linguistic hospitality "consists in transporting oneself into the linguistic domain of another, residing with the other, and bring the other back into one's own home as an invited guest."[26] This especially the case toward those areas of the planet that suffer most from climate change. International leaders have the task of both entering into the "linguistic domains" of the most fragile and to reside with them in that domain, sharing in their suffering. Analogously, or at least metaphorically, avoiding the negative anthropocentrism of anthropomorphizing the other-than-human world, those in power must become attentive to the suffering of the planet as well (understanding that from the suffering of the planet follows the suffering of humankind).

Alongside linguistic hospitality there arises narrative hospitality. Ricoeur writes: "at the very root of what we have just called linguistic hospitality, another sort of hospitality takes shape, which can be termed narrative hospitality, consisting in welcoming the history of others into my own history."[27] In the context of this chapter, Ricoeur is referring to various histories and founding events of different peoples that cannot (and should not be) substituted for one another—i.e., linguistic and narrative hospitality do not imply that the founding event and history of People X and those of People Y are interchangeable or that hospitality means People X receive the history of People Y as their own and vice versa. If founding events and histories do not remain distinct for those to whom they belong, then they can no longer constitute unique identities. In that case, the story itself is lost and there is no longer any "other" to whom to be hospitable or whom to welcome or with whom to exchange stories.

Where narrative hospitality takes place, however, stories are communicable, Ricoeur says. As such stories can be exchanged. Or, as Walter Benjamin beautifully puts it, the art of storying telling grants us "the ability to exchange experiences."[28] Kearney has written, likewise beautifully, that storytelling "gives us a *shareable world*.[29] So, while being conscious and attentive to the non-substitutability of our experiences, stories can be exchanged to the end of mutual understanding, healing, and to chart a way forward in peace. Ricoeur's description here, while in the context of memory and history, applies equally to telling the story of the future and exchanging visions and hopes for the future. And given that Ricoeur's reflections are built upon the work of Hans Jonas, there is explicitly a future dimension.

There are two ways this opens toward environmental philosophy and discourses in environmental justice. The first is toward the past. To move toward an "ethics of the future," the stories of past and present must be heard as well. Listening to the stories of those who can share what they have seen and experienced of environmental destruction as well as its direct effects of their lives, if welcomed in the sense of linguistic and narrative hospitality, we can begin to move in the direction of healing and justice. Healing and justice begin with recognition; but recognition is never something that is once for all attained. Ricoeur rightly explained: "The struggle for recognition perhaps remains endless. At the very least, the experience of actual recognition . . . confer on this struggle for recognition the assurance that the motivation which distinguishes it from the lust for power and shelters it from the fascination of violence is neither illusory nor vain."[30]

Obviously, exchanging stories and experiencing mutual recognition is not intended to remain in the past but to turn toward the future, which is the second contribution Ricoeur's thought makes to environmental philosophy and the discourses of environmental justice. There is one more element in this transition from the past to the future, which Ricoeur says springs from linguistic and narrative hospitality. It is "a third model of mediation, and thus of responsibility at the heart of the fragile" that "comes into view—the model of forgiveness."[31] It is here that while drawing on Ricoeur's account of the fragile and responsibility that I will deviate from him somewhat. What Ricoeur is suggesting is that in addition to exchanging stories, exchanging forgiveness is a necessary mediation. In the context of nations that have both suffered and caused suffering, the act of exchanging forgiveness is appropriate. What I would like to suggest here is that in the case of devastation to the environment and to the lives of those who have been disproportionately affected, those who have caused it are in the place of requesting forgiveness and the affected must be in a place to grant it. And, keep in mind, the larger context here is not exchanges between individuals, but larger institutional responsibility. So, rather than an exchange of forgiveness, the exchange is one of a request for forgiveness for an act of forgiving itself between perpetrators of environmental violence and the victims of it.

CONCLUSION

Ricoeur then asks whether forgiveness can be a category of the political. Ricoeur believes it can be. He writes: "I grant that here we are on the border of the political and the poetic, but it is good to know that politics, even at its most rigorous, remains political only if the rule of mutual recognition is able, in exceptional circumstances, to accept the infraction of forgiveness."[32] While Ricoeur here acknowledges the demarcation between the political and the poetic, he is right to point out their relation. It is the poetic that is key in turning toward the future, one that will make possible our survival as a species. The recognition of our fragility that leads us to acknowledge and take up our responsibility, will now turn toward a poetics. This poetics of environmental responsibility will be considered through Ricoeur's hermeneutics of imagination and initiative. This will be the subject matter of the next chapter.

NOTES

1. Secretariat of the Convention on Biological Diversity, "Message from Mr. Ahmed Djoghlaf, Executive Secretary, on the Occasion of the International Day for Biological

Diversity, 22 May 2007," https://www.cbd.int/doc/speech/2007/sp-2007-05-22-es-en .pdf.

2. John Bellamy Foster makes a strong argument for the retention of the term "Anthropocene" over "Capitalocene" on the basis of the meaning of the former in the natural sciences from whence to term came. To make "Capitalocene" the primary descriptive term for the age would "obliterate" the "fundamental scientific understanding" of the term "Anthropocene." Foster is clear that there is no doubt that capitalism is the cause of the birth of the Anthropocene. Thus, he argues that we should refer to "The Capitalinian" as the first geological age of the Anthropocene. See Foster's *Capitalism in the Anthropocene: Ecological Ruin or Ecological Revolution* (New York: Monthly Review Press, 2022), especially chapter 21, "The Capitalinian: The First Geological Age of the Anthropocene."

3. Paul Ricoeur, *Ethics, Politics, Ecology*," in his *Philosophy, Ethics, & Politics*, edited by Catherine Goldstein and translated by Kathleen Blamey (Cambridge, UK: Polity Press, 2020), 113.

4. Ian Angus, *Facing the Anthropocene: Fossil Capitalism and the Crisis of the Earth System*, foreword by John Bellamy Foster (New York: Monthly Review Press, 2016), 111.

5. Mark Fisher, *Capitalist Realism: Is There No Alternative?* (Washington: Zero Books, 2009), 15. Emphasis mine.

6. Foster, *Capitalism in the Anthropocene: Ecological Ruin or Ecological Revolution*, 363–64.

7. Keith R. Peterson, *A World Not Made for Us: Topics in Critical Environmental Philosophy* (Albany: SUNY Press, 2020), ix.

8. Peterson, *A World Not Made for Us*, 39.

9. Richard Kearney and Melissa Fitzpatrick, *Radical Hospitality: From Thought to Action* (New York: Fordham University Press, 2021), 108, 109.

10. Paul Ricoeur, "Responsibility and Fragility," in *Politics, Economy, and Society: Writings and Lectures, Volume 4*, translated by Kathleen Blamey (Cambridge, UK: Polity Press, 2021), 65–79.

11. Paul Ricoeur, *Politics, Economy, and Society*, 66.

12. Paul Ricoeur, *Politics, Economy, and Society*, 66.

13. Paul Ricoeur, *Politics, Economy, and Society*, 66.

14. Paul Ricoeur, *Politics, Economy, and Society*, 67.

15. Paul Ricoeur, *Politics, Economy, and Society*, 67.

16. Paul Ricoeur, *Politics, Economy, and Society*, 67–68.

17. Paul Ricoeur, *Politics, Economy, and Society*, 66.

18. Paul Ricoeur, *Politics, Economy, and Society*, 72.

19. Paul Ricoeur, *Politics, Economy, and Society*, 72.

20. See Hannah Arendt, "Understanding and Politics (The Difficulties of Understanding)" in *Essays in Understanding, 1930–1954: Formation, Exile, and Totalitarianism*, edited and with an introduction by Jerome Kohn (New York: Schocken Books, 1994), 307–27. On page 308, Arendt lamented those well-meaning individuals who wanted to use words as weapons as a shortcut through process of discourse, but that

"weapons and fighting belong in the realm of violence . . . violence begins where speech ends."

21. Paul Ricoeur, *Politics, Economy, and Society*, 73.

22. Paul Ricoeur, *Politics, Economy, and Society*, 73.

23. See Paul Ricoeur, *Philosophy, Ethics, and Politics*, edited by Catherine Goldenstein and translated by Kathleen Blamey (Cambridge, UK: Polity Press, 2020), 108.

24. I am grateful to Brian Gregor of California State University, Dominguez Hills, for suggestions that informed the content of this paragraph.

25. Paul Ricoeur, *Philosophy, Ethics, and Politics*, 106.

26. Paul Ricoeur, *Politics, Economy, and Society*, 74.

27. Paul Ricoeur, *Politics, Economy, and Society*, 75.

28. Walter Benjamin, "The Storyteller: Reflections on the Work of Nikolai Leskov," in *Illuminations: Essays and Reflections*, translated by Harry Zohn, edited and with an introduction by Hannah Arendt (New York: Schocken Books, 1968), 83.

29. Richard Kearney, *On Stories* (New York: Routledge, 2002), 3. Emphasis original.

30. Paul Ricoeur, *The Course of Recognition*, translated by David Pellauer (Cambridge, MA: Harvard University Press, 2005), 246.

31. Paul Ricoeur, *Politics, Economy, and Society*, 75.

32. Paul Ricoeur, *Politics, Economy, and Society*, 75.

Chapter 5

A Poetics of Environmental Responsibility

Imagination and Initiative

The preceding chapter addressed the concept of fragility as it pertains to threats to the environment and human life. Both the earth and human life are fragile. But the greater fragility is our own as we are vulnerable and dependent creatures, dependent upon the very earth that is being destroyed by human activity. To save fragile humanity from perishing, we must work to make the earth habitable. Ricoeur proposed that there exists an intrinsic connection between fragility and responsibility. He wrote that "responsibility has the fragile as its specific counterpart, that is to say, at once what is perishable to its natural weakness and what is threatened by the blows of political violence."[1] These notions, placed in the context of environmental catastrophe, would recognize the responsibility that we must take up in response to our own natural weakness, threatened by the blows of environmental violence (which surely also has its political element). Our asymmetric and utter dependence on the earth as spoken of in the preceding chapter makes our responsibility an imperative, not merely a suggestion.

The questions I take up in this chapter regard future action. In what sort of world do we wish to live? What sort of world do we wish to leave for those to come? On what grounds do we bring this world about? Once our present situation is recognized as environmentally precarious (if not a certain doom), we must ask ourselves what is required to change course. The fruits of the future will only grow from the roots of the present. Narratively considered, we need a change of plot, a change of story. Hence, a future that will turn the tide of environmental destruction in which we are implicated calls for a poetics of environmental responsibility. As responsibility, we must "respond" according to our "ability." What can be done must be done for the sake of the continuation of human life. The cost of doing nothing is too high, and we do not have the ability to pay. As a poetics, our responsibility is forward-looking; it is world-creating. I will explore these questions in the light of Ricoeur's hermeneutics of imagination and initiative. Action (initiative) is required to meet the demands of the environmental crisis, and imagination is the source of the content of action.

HUMAN EXCEPTIONALISM AND RESPONSIBILITY

Having understood our fragility and vulnerability, we must awaken fully to the imperative of responsibility.[2] Responsibility comes from our capacity to act. Capable human being is responsible human being. Agency and responsibility cannot be separated. Moreover, responsibility cannot be separated from what is distinctive about humans, or what might be called "human exceptionalism." This requires some explanation. In environmental ethics, "human exceptionalism" is typically frowned upon as it is taken to mean human superiority. Viewing ourselves as superior, after all, has been the basis for so much environmental exploitation. If we are the superior creatures, it is thought that the subjugation of lower creatures is not morally wrong. The entire history of the environmental movement is predicated on the notion that the root of all environmental devastation is the belief in the centrality and superiority of the human species; hence, the designation of "anthropocentrism" as negative and the source of environmental harm.

Might we consider a different meaning of "human exceptionalism" that does not imply superiority? In one sense, "exceptionalism" simply refers to what is unique in character to something. As Ricoeur used the term "exceptionalism," referred to in chapter 1, he simply intended the capacities unique to humans. Specifically, he referred to our capacity to question as well as noting that we are uniquely endowed with "knowledge and responsibility."[3] Other animals do not ask whether any other beings possess intrinsic value, if rivers have rights, or about the effects of their activities on the climate. This is why Ricoeur referred in that passage to our capacity to question as both a "privilege and a curse." Because we can question, because we can acquire knowledge and understanding, we are uniquely burdened with responsibility for the world about which we inquire and in which we act. Exceptionalism in this sense is not a privileged superiority. Rather, it carries the weight of responsibility in thought and action. As human beings, we dwell in the constant tension between being a part of the ecosystem (a "fragment" as Ricoeur said) while simultaneously possessing capacities unique to our species. It is precisely these unique capacities that set us apart and bestow upon us environmental responsibility. Our exceptionalism (mere difference) must not be denied but reframed in terms of its connection to responsibility.

POETICS AND RESPONSIBILITY

May we refer to the future as hermeneutical? That is, can we interpret the future? At the end of the preceding chapter, I noted the link that Ricoeur made between the political and the poetic. What we do (action) is itself an interpretation, a response to how we understand the past and the present; but action is always oriented—thrusts itself forward—toward the world to be. When we act, we are moving toward something that is not-yet that we intend to be. "[H]uman action is always oriented toward a future state of affairs or world that they aim to bring about."[4] Our environmental future is an interpretation that comes in the form of what we envision as a world in which we wish to live. Political action (which I argued in the preceding chapter is necessary for the implementation of environmental change) will be carried out both as a response to an evaluation of the past and present but is always thrust forward to create the world we envision.

Richard Kearney has pointed out that Ricoeur's hermeneutics of the past reminds us that "history is more than what has taken place; it involves 'potential' unrealized aspirations still dormant in the past."[5] Similarly, with regard to metaphor, Charles Reagan, in his biography of Ricoeur, wrote: "Metaphors give us a new way to describe, a redescription, of the world, just as the interpretation of texts presents to us a world which could be our world, and . . . the world in which I live and the world in which I could live."[6] Interpretation is a dialectic between past and present on the one hand and the future on the other. What this means for environmental hermeneutics is that, in light of the connection between fragility and responsibility, responsibility tends toward the future. It means considering potential worlds to which we aspire that becomes the basis for action. The imperative of responsibility calls forth a poetics. In fact, it is the ethical vision of Hans Jonas[7] that Ricoeur explicitly draws upon and which is entirely aimed at the future.

I think here again of the heuristic of fear discussed in chapter 1. By considering dangers that are possible, even if improbable, we seek to avoid negative and catastrophic outcomes. We want to be clear about what we do not want in our future. But is not what we do not want understood both in terms of evil that we wish to avoid and, if not more so, the good that we seek to bring about? In other words, do we not already envision potential worlds that we hope to be when we consider, with the heuristic of fear, things incompatible with those worlds? So, if our fragility is the root of responsibility, and responsibility is oriented toward the future, then our responsibility is, likewise, a poetics.

Ricoeur mentions the dual sense of the word "poetics." One being "creativity on the plane of the dynamics of action" and the other "song and hymn on the plane of verbal expression."[8] It is this first sense that pertains most to a poetics of environmental responsibility. "Poetics" has its root in the Greek poiesis, which means to "make" or to "bring forth." A poetics of environmental responsibility, therefore, refers to our responsibility to create a world that is environmentally healthy and one that is environmentally just to all peoples, globally. Furthermore, as a poetics, we must be creative, both in the sense of creating a new world in which we would want to live and in the sense of creative solutions brought forth from the depths of imagination. Ricoeur, from the quotation above, links creativity to action. Likewise, he links imagination to action. He links both to poetics. For Ricoeur, the poetical imagination and practice are two sides of the same coin.

IMAGINATION AND A POETICS OF
ENVIRONMENTAL RESPONSIBILITY

Ricoeur's theory of imagination is part of a larger "investigation" that he refers to as a "poetics of the will."[9] He insists that "the best test of its [a theory's] claim to universality lay in determining its capacity for extension to the sphere of practice."[10] Ricoeur's theory of imagination is situated within language. What he will call the "semantic innovation" will provide the model from moving from theory to practice. In order to develop the idea of imagination as a tool that brings about solutions and action, Ricoeur first must defend the idea of image against its detractors. He must overcome the "bad reputation" from which imagination has suffered.

First, imagination may refer to things that are absent and, in the case, say for example, of art, have "their own physical existence, but whose function is to 'take the place of' the things they represent."[11] Beyond that, an image can also refer, not merely to absent and existing things, but to things that do not exist at all. As such, the image possesses only a "pure literary existence" and is, therefore, a fiction. In either case, however imagination is conceived, it is weaker than the real and the present. Ricoeur's response to this was what he called the productive imagination. Combine imagination's evocation of the absent with a "critical consciousness of the difference between the imaginary and the real" and you have a productive imagination.[12] Absent the critical consciousness, the imaginary and the real are indistinguishable. However, with critical consciousness, "imagination is the very instrument of the critique of the real."[13]

Can imagination be a source of critique of the very real environmental challenges humanity is facing? It would seem safe to say that whether the future holds a reversal of the environmental course we are presently on or if we remain on this current course to our own demise, it will be the function of imagination. A critical environmental imagination will propose a world free of environmental injustice and one in which the planet is interpreted otherwise than a pool of resources to exploit. And, as was highlighted in the previous chapter, such a critical environmental imagination is going to require international, cooperative, and collaborative institutions and actionable agreements among nations. The reason imagination will have to work and influence on this level is that the source(s) of our environmental problems are on that level.

What sort of critical environmental imaginings are necessary? The apt title of a recent collection of essays edited by Martin Empson sums it up, *System Change Not Climate Change*.[14] Empson and the other contributors argue that the systemic problem is the capitalist system, whether that be capitalism's addiction to fossil fuel or its impact on things such as agriculture. The sheer number of books in just the last few years that represent imaginative critique of the capitalist system as the root of the climate crisis are too many to number.[15] One tenet that they all share is that a system overhaul must be international. Empson, in his introduction to the book just mentioned, cites the recent report of IPCC, which insists that what is needed to keep the rise of the global temperature in check is no less than "transformative systemic change."[16]

The "critique of the real," it goes without saying, is for the purpose of changing the real from what it is in favor of a new real that we desire to create. Critical consciousness is the first step in this process, but it does not end there. What is next in the process of poetically "imaging" a new world to unfold in front of our understanding? For Ricoeur, the answer lies in discourse and what he calls the "semantic innovation," which is to say to derive the image from language. Ricoeur notes the challenge that is presented in the semantic innovation insofar as, traditionally, "so many prejudices have been tied to the idea that the image is an appendix to perception, a shadow of perception."[17] How is it then that language is source of the image?

There are specific reasons why this might also be perceived as a problem for environmental hermeneutics. After all, the environment, the so-called "natural world," is material. I argued in chapter 2 that environmental identity is in the flesh, that is, corporeal contact with the earth. Would it not be the case that the image/imagination with regard to the environment be definitively tied to sense perception? How could environmental imagination be rooted in language? I suggest two ways. The first is that, like most dualisms (especially the mind-body dualism), making a dualism between flesh and language limits and obscures understanding. The second is that a poetics of environmental responsibility is future oriented, that is, turned toward a world that does not yet exist but waiting to be created. While past and present images of the environment are certainly mediated in the flesh, it can only be in language (especially in the form of discourse) that the future can be conceived and then brought about, a sort of word-made-flesh. I will consider each of these in turn.

While it is true that sense perception is constituent of our relationship to our environment, we must be careful not to make what is a distinction between language and flesh into a gulf between them. For even language is mediated in the flesh. Whether it is speech that is expressed and heard or the ink of text upon a page, the language event happens in bodies. The thoughts of our minds are expressed through our bodies. As "incarnate Cogitos," Ricoeur reminds us, for example, that the "body is the most basic source of motives," that values "enter history through my body," and that it is "the personal body in which Cogito shares as its very existence."[18] Language may be the house of Being, as Heidegger said,[19] but the body is the house of language. The body/flesh serves as mediator both for our lived experience of the environment and for the language in which experience is understood and articulated. The body is the common link between the two. Language and flesh are distinct, but they are not separate. To separate them and create a dualism is to deny the embodied nature of language and the linguisticality of the body. Hence, language can be a source of the environmental image, but this is most evident in the future orientation of the poetics of environmental responsibility. Environmental responsibility, as has been said, is about an ethics of the future. It is in discourse that "our images are spoken before they are seen,"[20] and, therefore, not an "appendix" or "shadow" of perception. Rather, the image is a projection forward to be realized and actualized in the future—that is, to be embodied.

Ricoeur begins his own response to the question of how the image derives from language by turning to the poetic image. "The poet is the artisan of language who engenders and shapes images through language alone." Thus: "Before being a fading perception, the image is an emerging meaning."[21] As to the emergence of meaning, Ricoeur defines imagination as "the free play of possibilities in a state of noninvolvement with respect to the world of perception or of action. It is in this state of noninvolvement that we try out new ideas, new values, new ways of being in the world."[22] What Ricoeur wishes for us not to forget is that images, being engendered and shaped by language, are first heard (discourse) before being seen. To illustrate this, Ricoeur turns to what he calls the heuristic force of fiction. Just as the heuristic of fear bids us to consider all potential harmful consequences of our actions, and thus avoid those actions, the heuristic power of fiction, in that free play of possibilities, allows us to imagine new realities.

At first glance, because fiction seems to point only to "nonplace," the words can only have sense (meaning) but not reference (to concrete reality). But, when considered as the exercise of imagination toward the world to come, Ricoeur says that within fiction it is now possible to "transition from sense to reference." The "reference-effect" of fiction is precisely in its power to "redescribe reality."[23] For environmental discourse, it can be understood that the future is, as yet, nonbeing—or better yet, the future is a becoming, an unfolding of being. Imagination, therefore, is simultaneously a critique of the real (as noted above) and the place from which reality can be redescribed,[24] which becomes the basis of action (action that will determine what comes into being). Ricoeur writes: "It is imagination that provides the milieu, the luminous clearing, in which we can compare and evaluate motives as diverse as desires and ethical obligations. "[25] We can, in imagination, consider what our actions might lead to, why we would choose one path over another, what our duties are and whether our actions fulfill our duties or run contrary to them.

The point of environmental discourse is to engender environmental imagination to the end of motivating environmental action. A Ricoeurian environmental hermeneutics proposes the importance of imagination. Why? If Steven Vogel is correct that our practices (actions) produce or create our environment,[26] we must realize that the imagination produces our practices, and it is language (discourse) that produces the image. What is important to point out here is that the world to come will indeed come, but it will not do so entirely on its own. The world to come will be a world that was imagined. The pressing importance of environmental discourse lies in this fact. The responsibility toward our environmental future is a poetic one.

INITIATIVE AND THE POETICS OF
ENVIRONMENTAL RESPONSIBILITY

As imagination moves to practice, I turn now to Ricoeur's analysis of initiative. For Ricoeur, initiative is practical with "ethical and political extensions."[27] Initiative will further illuminate the future orientation of environmental responsibility in its relationship to past and present. Ricoeur chose the term "initiative," and defines it as "the living active, operative present-answering to the present that is gazed upon, considered, contemplated, reflected."[28] The present upon which we are gazing, considering, contemplating, and reflecting is the environmental crisis with which we are faced. This present requires a response. It requires initiative.

The present, Ricoeur says, appears to be in a middle position situated between the past and the future in an oppositional relation. When we think of the present, it is a now in front of what is now identified as past. We also think of the present as a now relative to a future that will unfold. From our place in the present, we turn to the past, which takes the form of things such as "memory, regret, remorse, commemoration, or loathing." Likewise, from our place in the present we turn toward the future with "desire, fear, expectation, and flight."[29] These and other things that might be listed as to our present relationship to past and future can be placed under the umbrella of memory and expectation. To turn to the past is to remember what has been and the turn to the future is an expectation of what will be. Initiative (action) can only take place in the present. The initiative that I take arises out of this sort of dialectic between memory and expectation. In this sense, Ricoeur says, the present serves as both an origin and as transit. The present is origin "in the sense that future and past appear as horizons projected ahead of and behind a present" and a transit "in the sense that the future things we dread or desire come closer as it were to the present, cross through it, and then move away from us sinking behind in memory, which will soon become oblivion."[30] With the past, being memory, we can only reflect and "learn from the past" as it were, but the past can also inform present initiative designed to create the future we poetically imagine.

ENVIRONMENTAL JUSTICE
INTERLUDE: HERITAGE AND FUTURE

Here I wish to briefly discuss what this might mean for environmental justice, especially as it relates to environmental identity and environmental heritage. Robert Figueroa, a leading environmental justice scholar, defines environmental identity as "the amalgamation of cultural identities, ways of life, and self-perceptions that are connected to a given group's physical environment."[31] Related to environmental identity is environmental heritage. Figueroa writes: "Environmental identity is closely related to environmental heritage, where the meaning and symbols of the past frame values, practices, and places we wish to preserve for ourselves as members of a community. In other words, our environmental heritage is our environmental identity in relation to a community viewed over time."[32] Memory is more than just remembering a past, it is constituent of present and future identity and a living heritage. In terms of expectation, a community asks "what will our future be, what will become of us"? The nature of the present as transit is crucial for environmental justice. The past, present, and future are not separated designations of time, but constitute connected movement through time. Justice would demand that a community whose identity and heritage, which is connected to their environment, to the extent possible, be self-determining with regard to their future. Thus, any environmental impact stemming from human action that will affect a community should hear the voices of that community, and their environmental identities and heritages should guide any decision-making.

Taking environmental heritage into account is an act of narrative hospitality (see chapter 4, note 26). One purpose of narrative hospitality in these instances is to avoid creating what Ricoeur calls a "discordance" in the narrative process. Ricoeur defines "discordance" as "the reversals of fortune that make the plot an ordered transformation to a terminal situation."[33] A community's narrative is a movement from the past, through the present, into their future. When anything disrupts the desired trajectory of that narrative movement, where an unexpected change in the plot occurs, the unifying concordance of the narrative is disrupted. Many discordances are outside human control. In the path of life, sometimes things simply happen. But a discordance, a reversal of fortune, that befalls a community due to the actions of others and disrupts their narrative by doing harm to their environment is an instance of environmental injustice. Hence, in initiative as Ricoeur has been describing it, the dialectic between origin and transit in the present instant operates as a hermeneutic guide to our poetics of environmental responsibility.

Beyond instances of environmental injustice as it pertains to particular communities, we must recall the global scale of environmental harm. While, for example, climate change does impact different places on the globe differently and with differing degrees of harm, ultimately we will be faced with an uninhabitable planet threatening the extinction of the entire human species. So, it is clear that the Ricoeurian concept of initiative must be applied broadly to myriad regional or individual instances as well as on the global scale. In each case, the ultimate end is the same—to take ethical responsibility for the outcomes of human action with the aim of creating a world that is just, habitable, and enduring.

INITIATIVE, NARRATIVE, RESPONSIBILITY, AND THE ETHICS OF THE PROMISE

There is a very close relationship between Ricoeur's reflections on initiative and that of his narrative hermeneutics, which in turn is connected to the ethical life, all of which provide a framework to address the environmental crisis. Let us recall Ricoeur's definition of initiative cited earlier as "the living, active, operative present answering to the present that is gazed upon, considered, contemplated, reflected" (see note 25). The present is understood in an oppositional relation to past and future that functions as both origin and transit, memory, and expectation. This aligns closely with the characteristics of narrative, namely prefiguration, configuration, and refiguration. Just as there is a received past and a present upon which we gaze, consider, contemplate, and reflect as we look forward into our future, there is narrative prefiguration, configuration, and refiguration that correspond.

Prefiguration (also referred to as mimesis₁) is the world in which we find ourselves, into which we were thrown, and which provide a pre-understanding of the world. Ricoeur says that "the composition of the plot is grounded in a pre-understanding of the world of action, its meaningful structures, its symbolic resources, and its temporal character."[34] And: "If, in fact, human action can be narrated, it is because it is always already articulated by signs, rules, and norms. It is always already symbolically mediated."[35] The prefigured world is likened to the past as origin, which we find ourselves in within the present. It is this past that has given us language, cultural norms and customs, and the social-political structures that give us a sense of self.

What do we do then with all the parts of the prefigured world? This is the step of configuration, or mimesis₂, that "opens the kingdom of the as if."[36] What is configured at this stage are all the disparate parts of the prefigured world, that is, through what Ricoeur calls "emplotment," things such as persons or events are mediated by configuration in order to create (that is, narrate) a coherent, meaningful story. In terms of initiative, we are contemplating and reflecting upon our present in order to give it a sense of meaning. Why else would we be contemplating and reflecting other than to interpret the present, that is, to understand it? Configuration is now a necessary transitory instant that turns from the prefigured past to the future. Linking this move to imagination and poetics, we ask ourselves what sort of world do we want to live in? What kind of people do we wish to be in that world? Configuration is the bridge that links memory to expectation and, as narration, configuration mediates between them.

Mimesis₃, or refiguration, is the turn toward the not-yet, but what could be. Ricoeur writes that "the expectation of the future is inscribed in the present; it is the future-become-present, turned toward the not-yet."[37] Ricoeur describes this as the horizon of expectation as to what could be, which becomes the poetically imagined world we act to bring about. Expectation includes desire and hope, which becomes what motivates us, standing in our configured world, to begin to refigure it. Over time, and speaking generationally, the refigured world for one generation becomes the prefigured world for the next. The environmental crisis that we now contemplate in the present has an origin. There is a sense that coming into this day and time in history, we come into a prefigured world of human action and decision-making that has placed us in the position we stand in now, environmentally. From our standpoint in the present, we must bring together (configure) via emplotment, all of the various aspects of the environmental crisis and then turn toward the not-yet, but what may be.

Finally, we come now to responsibility and ethics. These are akin ethical aspects to both initiative and narrative. I begin with narrative. Another way to think of the three stages of mimesis—prefiguration, configuration, and refiguration—is to say "describe, narrate, prescribe."[38] Narrative (configuration) mediates between description and prescription, Ricoeur says, when we anticipate that "ethical considerations are implied in the very structure of the act of narrating" and recognized that "there is no ethically neutral narrative."[39] The stage of configuring the prefigured world assumes certain values and judgments. How we bring the parts together and what we interpret that it means for the future is a moral judgment. Hence, we speak of the moral of the story. This becomes all the more evident when we consider that refiguring involves actions behind which are values, moral attitudes and beliefs, and judgments. One does not set about refiguring in any ethically neutral way. Rather, what actions are chosen, what is imagined to bring forth, reflect an ethical orientation. Refiguration and ethical prescription in this sense are one and the same.

This raises the question: "What ethical orientation must guide what we prescribe"? After all, prescription that comes out a wanting ethics can only lead to harm. Environmentally speaking, I would say that our ethical orientation be one that is motivated by the polycentric ethics I covered in chapter 3, which also implies a communal aspect. As I have mentioned several times throughout this text, Ricoeur rightly spoke of the hermeneutical tension between being a fragment of the ecosystem, yet its own distinct part. Recognizing that every fragment of the ecosystem is simultaneously a distinct part and belonging to the whole. This hermeneutical tension created by several parts that constitute a whole must be carefully navigated and, especially, adjudicated. The end aim, again, is a habitable world.

Ricoeur's "ethical aim" or "ethical intention" is defined by him as "aiming at the 'good life' with and for others, in just institutions."[40] The ethical aim has two highly important characteristics: that it is social and, with institutions, political. Now, an important question is whether the "others" of the ethical intention can be nonhuman others. This is certainly contestable. My response is simply that it may not matter. Why? One reason is that any possibility of the good life for humans requires an environment that can sustain us. So even if we say the ethical intention can only apply to human beings (as moral creatures) our good, as individuals and as a community, is utterly contingent upon an inhabitable environment. So, aiming at the good life must include sound environmental policy. Further, sound environmental policy must be institutionalized, and the institutions must be just. The good life for each individual must be protected, yet each of us must pursue the good life both with others and for others, recognizing that there is no good life for me that is just and meaningful in any sense unless there is also a good life for you. Therefore, I pursue the good life alongside you and, just as importantly if not more, that I pursue it for you. And for that to be successful, it must be embodied in just institutions. It should be noncontroversial to say that any genuine fulfillment of the ethical aim must invariably include the environment, regardless of how that might be conceived. For, without an environment, there is no dwelling. In pursuit of the good life, the better and more hospitable the environment, the greater the potential to attain and enjoy the good life.

For initiative, Ricoeur writes: "To speak of initiative is to speak of responsibility."[41] We now return to our central theme of responsibility. Initiative and responsibility are intertwined because initiative is about doing, it is about action. Our fragility requires responsibility, and responsibility demands action, that is, initiative. Ricoeur writes: "No longer attending to what happens but to what we make happen."[42] While there is an aspect of passivity and the involuntary, agency still remains. Speaking of the body as the locus of powers and nonpowers, Ricoeur says of the "possibilities of the flesh" that: "The notion of circumstance is articulated here on that of powers and nonpowers, as that which surrounds my power of acting, offering the counterpart of obstacles or of workable paths for the exercise of my powers."[43] Perhaps these words can be restated to say that my power of acting, the voluntary, is surrounded by the involuntary, but the voluntary has the capacity to negotiate those "workable paths" in addressing environmental crises. As beings with agency, we have responsibility to the extent that we have the capacity and potential to act.

But, how is this capacity to be mobilized? This is where Ricoeur comes back to an idea related to semantic innovation,[44] which he refers to as the semantics of action. The semantics of action is "the conceptual network in which we articulate the order of human action: projects, intentions, motives, circumstances, intended or unintended effects, and so on." Ricoeur does not say so here, but I would take the semantics of action, especially as it pertains to addressing the environmental crisis, as being able to refer back to what was said already about linguistic hospitality and narrative. In the context of addressing environmental problems, the ability to articulate the poetics of environmental responsibility collectively and collaboratively would seem to be a necessary component of success. A rather simple way to articulate this is simply to say we must dialogue, and that dialogue should take place between affected peoples, philosophers, sociologists, psychologists (especially environmental psychologists), biologists, ecologists, and any and all academic disciplines that have something to contribute. This conversation should extend to the political sphere as leaders need to take seriously the fragility of the human species and the consequences of their decisions for the future of the human species. Lastly, academics should also act as advisors to the general population. Beyond doing research confined within our own disciplines and university halls, the environmental crisis demands that we write and speak to all people rather than just the parochial confines of our peers.

I wish to conclude this section with one last consideration. Following Ricoeur's words that the speech of initiative is coextensive with that of responsibility, I want to mention what he then said about the speech act of promising. He wrote: "The promise, I shall say, is the ethics of initiative. The heart of this ethics is the promise to keep my promises. Being faithful to one's word thus becomes a guarantee that the beginning will have a sequel, that the initiative will actually inaugurate a new course of things."[45] If the environment is to be able to sustain human life, a promise is needed on the part of those with the power to bring change about. Initiative that will "actually inaugurate a new course of things" cannot be accepted on the basis of words alone, but words that are a promise. This is the ethical demand of initiative. And this is the heart of a poetics of responsibility.

CONCLUSION

The preceding chapter and this one constitutes two parts of one whole. There is an uninterrupted flow from fragility to responsibility to action. From the recognition of fragility flows the imperative of responsibility. Out of responsibility flows the necessity of a poetics of imagination that, in turn, flows into initiative from which guides action to the end of bringing solutions to the environmental crisis. If we choose to survive, we must also choose how we are to be in the not-yet, but the future-become-present that will inevitably be. What is certain is that if we do not muster the imagination and take the initiative to change course, these questions will no longer matter.

NOTES

1. Paul Ricoeur, *Politics, Economy, and Society: Writings and Lectures, Volume 4*, translated by Kathleen Blamey (Cambridge, UK: Polity Press, 2021), 66.

2. I am using the phrase "imperative of responsibility" from the title of the text by Hans Jonas, *The Imperative of Responsibility*, to which Ricoeur refers in the interview that was the subject of the first chapter as well as in Ricoeur's text *The Course of Recognition*. See notes 17 and 31 from chapter 1.

3. See Paul Ricoeur, *Philosophy, Ethics, & Politics*, edited by Catherine Goldenstein and translated by Kathleen Blamey (Cambridge, UK: Polity Press, 2020), 113.

4. Melissa Fitzpatrick, "Telelogical Hospitality: The Case of Contemporary Virtue Ethics," in Richard Kearney and Melissa Fitzpatrick, *Radical Hospitality: From Thought to Action* (New York: Fordham University Press, 2021), 90.

5. Richard Kearney, "Narrative Hospitality: Three Pedagogical Experiments," in Richard Kearney and Melissa Fitzpatrick, *Radical Hospitality: From Thought to Action* (New York: Fordham University Press, 2021), 33.

6. Charles E. Reagan, *Paul Ricoeur: His Life and Work* (Chicago: University of Chicago Press, 1996), 43.

7. I refer the reader to Jonas's *The Imperative of Responsibility* (see the bibliography), especially chapter 2, "On Principles and Method," where Jonas speaks of an "ethics of the future" as well as first delineating the "heuristic of fear," and chapter 5, "Responsibility Today: Endangered Future and the Idea of Progress." It is in chapter 5 where Jonas speaks of the future of nature and that of humankind, no doubt from where Ricoeur formulated the phrase, quoted several times in this text, "for there to be humanity after us, there has to be nature after us." See note 38 in chapter 1.

8. Ricoeur, *Politics, Economy, and Society*, 178.

9. Paul Ricoeur, *From Text to Action: Essays in Hermeneutics II*, translated by Kathleen Blamey and John B. Thompson (Evanston, IL: Northwestern University Press, 1991), 168. For a briefer discussion on Ricoeur's theory of imagination as it applies to environmental discourse, see David Utsler and Cynthia R. Nielsen, "(Environmental) Hermeneutics at the Heart of the Anthropocene," in *Analecta Hermeneutica* 13 (2021): 53–72.

10. Ricoeur, *From Text to Action*, 168.

11. Ricoeur, *From Text to Action*, 170.

12. Ricoeur, *From Text to Action*, 170.

13. Ricoeur, *From Text to Action*, 171.

14. Martin Empson, ed., *System Change Not Climate Change* (London: Bookmarks Publications, 2019).

15. See for example: Ian Angus, *Facing the Anthropocene: Fossil Capitalism and the Crisis of the Earth System* (New York: Monthly Review Press, 2016; Martin Empson, ed. *System Change*; John Bellamy Foster, *Capitalism in the Anthropocene: Ecological Ruin or Ecological Revolution* (New York: Monthly Review Press, 2022). Matthew T. Huber, *Climate Change as Class War: Building Socialism on a Warming Planet* (London: Verso, 2022); Naomi Klein, *This Changes Everything: Capitalism vs. the Climate* (New York: Simon & Schuster, 2014); Andreas Malm, *Fossil Capital: The Rise of Steam Power and the Roots of Global Warming* (London: Verso, 2016).

16. Empson, *Systemic Change*, 8.

17. Ricoeur, *From Text to Action*, 171.

18. Paul Ricoeur, *Freedom and Nature: The Voluntary and the Involuntary*, translated by Erazim V. Kohák (Evanston, IL: Northwestern University Press, 1966), 85, 88.

19. Martin Heidegger, "Letter on Humanism," in *Basic Writings* (New York: Harper Perennial Modern Thought, 2008), 217.

20. Ricoeur, *From Text to Action*, 171.

21. Ricoeur, *From Text to Action*, 173.

22. Ricoeur, *From Text to Action*, 174.

23. Ricoeur, *From Text to Action*, 175. Emphasis original.

24. In his recent book on Herbert Marcuse, Andrew Feenberg refers to Marcuse's thought on the gap between the real and the potential, expressing in an illuminating way what I understand Ricoeur to be saying. Feenberg writes: "Consciousness of

social potentialities must be attributed to the imagination because it alone has the power to project beyond the given toward an ideal form. Marcuse argues that the imagination is an essential aspect of rationality since it directs the subject toward a valid, if unrealized dimension of the experienced world. . . . The imagination is a psychological faculty as well as a source of insight into reality. . . . The gap between imagined fulfillment . . . and the actual condition of particular beings is the stimulus of development. Life is perpetually engaged in overcoming that gap through transforming the environment and absorbing it into the world of the self." See Andrew Feenberg, *The Ruthless Critique of Everything Existing: Nature and Revolution in Marcuse's Philosophy of Praxis* (Brooklyn: Verso Books, 2023), xiv–xv. Beyond the similarity between Ricoeur and Marcuse regarding imagination as a means of envisioning potentialities, an interesting line of inquiry (outside the scope of the present work) would be Ricoeur's mediation of "ideology and utopia" and the development of his "critical hermeneutics" that, to my mind, go beyond the critique of ideology in Marcuse and early critical theory generally and would plumb even more deeply into the necessity of imagination for working toward a habitable earth and our environmental future.

25. Ricoeur, *From Text to Action*, 177.
26. Vogel makes this argument throughout his book *Thinking Like a Mall: Environmental Philosophy After the End of Nature* (Cambridge, MA: MIT Press, 2016).
27. Ricoeur, *From Text to Action*, 208.
28. Ricoeur, *From Text to Action*, 208.
29. Ricouer, *From Text to Action*, 209.
30. Ricoeur, *From Text to Action*, 209.
31. Robert Melchior Figueroa, "Evaluating Environmental Justice Claims," in *Forging Environmentalism: Justice, Livelihood and Contested Environments*, ed. Joanne Bauer (New York: M.E. Sharpe, 2006), 371.
32. Figueroa, 372.
33. Paul Ricoeur, *Oneself as Another*, translated by Kathleen Blamey (Chicago: University of Chicago Press, 1992), 141.
34. Paul Ricoeur, *Time and Narrative. Vol. I*, translated by Kathleen Blamey and David Pellauer (Chicago: University of Chicago Press, 1984), 54.
35. Paul Ricoeur, *Time and Narrative, Vol. I*, 57.
36. Paul Ricoeur, *Time and Narrative, Vol. I*, 64. Emphasis original.
37. Paul Ricoeur, *From Text to Action*, 218. Emphasis original.
38. Paul Ricoeur, *Oneself as Another*, 114.
39. Paul Ricoeur, *Oneself as Another*, 115.
40. Paul Ricoeur, *Oneself as Another*, 172. For another reading of Ricoeur's ethical aim as applied to the environment, see Nathan Bell, "Environmental Hermeneutics with and for Others: Ricoeur's Ethics and the Ecological Self," in *Interpreting Nature: The Emerging Field of Environmental Hermeneutics*, edited by Forrest Clingerman, et al. (New York: Fordham University Press, 2014) 141–59.
41. Paul Ricoeur, *From Text to Action*, 217.

42. Paul Ricoeur, *From Text to Action*, 215.
43. Paul Ricoeur, *From Text to Action*, 215.
44. Paul Ricoeur, *From Text to Action*, 215–16.
45. Paul Ricoeur, *From Text to Action*, 217. Emphasis mine.

Chapter 6

Is Interpreting Nature to Read It as a Text?

Writing a book on environmental hermeneutics derived from the philosophy of Paul Ricoeur and failing to address Ricoeur's turn to the text would be a substantial omission. At first glance, a Ricoeurian environmental hermeneutics would seem to suggest that interpreting environments is akin to interpreting texts. The text becomes a metaphor[1] when interpretation turns toward non-texts, such as works of art, landscapes, film, or any object of interpretation. While it is the case that the interpretation of texts is deeply rooted in the original practice of hermeneutics and forms a significant part of its history and meaning, hermeneutics must be understood more broadly as the study of the fundamental human activity of interpreting. A text is but one thing among many that can be interpreted and understood, and there is no necessary reason to have to imagine an environment as a book to interpret it, that is, to engage in the work of understanding it. In fact, to imagine an environment as something it is not—a text—would seem to limit the scope and potential of how it can be understood. The environment must be taken on its own "terms" and in its own being for the purposes of interpretation.

In the case of an explicitly Ricoeurian environmental hermeneutics, then, Ricoeur's text-centric hermeneutics cannot be ignored. Ricoeur explicitly provided a working definition of hermeneutics as "the theory of the operations of understanding in their relation to the interpretation of texts."[2] It would be all too easy to fall back on an analogy and say that with the hermeneutic theories of text interpretation we are "reading" environments. It would be easy, but it would also detract from the more general scope of hermeneutical experience. What I will argue in this chapter is that even Ricoeur's text-centric hermeneutics can be understood as a subset of a more general theory of interpretation. Further, I will argue that when we look at other aspects of Ricoeur's hermeneutics that are not focused on text interpretation, especially his return to the body, for example, we can identify Ricoeur's overall hermeneutics as operating within a general understanding of hermeneutical experience.

THE BOOK OF NATURE

The idea of nature as a text to be read, a "book of nature," is many centuries old.[3] While the sacred text, the Word of God in written form, serves as a media of divine revelation, the natural world was also seen as a medium of divine disclosure. I do not mean to say that referring to the book of nature, or any version of the metaphor of the text, is in any sense a strict error. As human beings we tend to gain deeper understandings of things with the use of metaphor. When we speak of reading nature, it is implicit that the word "reading" simply means "understanding," such as when we say we have a "read" on something. When we ask someone if we are "reading" them correctly, we are asking them if we rightly understand what they are saying to us.

Why is the metaphor of "reading" so appealing to us? One reason, I suspect, is that we are language beings. Gadamer has famously said that "being that can be understood is language"[4] and asserts that language is our medium of understanding. He has gone even further to express that language is universal and all-encompassing: "Language is not a delimited realm of the speakable, over against which other realms that are unspeakable might stand. Rather, language is all encompassing. There is nothing that is fundamentally excluded from being said, to the extent that our act of meaning intends."[5] Anytime we understand anything at all, that understanding is articulated in language. Most certainly, language is a necessary requirement for discourse and shared understanding. Hermeneutical experiences, such as an encounter with the other-than-human world, are not themselves linguistic and they can rightly be called prelinguistic. But even prelinguistic is truly "pre" or before in the sense that descriptive language follows hermeneutical experience through which we understand the experience in reflection. Written texts represent one modality of language and, because we are language beings, we are comfortable in the metaphor of the text and that of reading.

A distinction must be made here, however, between a text as something which we read and interpret versus language as the place where being is understood. This distinction is crucial for a proper understanding of the metaphor of the text and why interpreting "nature" or environments are better not thought of as texts to be read. In the case of the hermeneutics of the text, it is the text that is the object of interpretation. A text ("any discourse fixed by writing" as Ricoeur has defined it[6]) is read with the intent to understand its meaning(s). Text interpretation is to read written language. It is written language itself, the discourse fixed by writing, that is the object of hermeneutical inquiry. This is distinct from the use of language to articulate an understanding of any hermeneutical experience. Language in this case, in the Gadamerian sense, is not itself the object of hermeneutical inquiry, but the medium through which we understand the object of hermeneutical inquiry whatever that may be—text, work of art, nature, or anything that we seek to understand. All hermeneutical experience is "speakable," as Gadamer says.

When we speak of the metaphor or model of the text, the underlying assumption is that hermeneutics is fundamentally about interpreting texts, so when seeking to understand things other than texts, such as "nature," we just think of it as a text—that is, the "book of nature." While such is not necessarily problematic in itself and fine to some extent, the metaphor of the text does present limitations on the ways in which we encounter the world in hermeneutical experience. One reason involves the senses. Actual reading involves only the sense of sight. But different hermeneutical experiences engage other senses, so limiting general interpretive experiences to the metaphor of the text can obscure the "surplus of meaning" to be discovered. As recent work in the area of "carnal hermeneutics" has convincingly argued, the body is interpretation.[7] Despite the fact that hermeneutical understanding is articulated in language, as a sort of second order reflection on experience, the first order is the embodied experience itself in which interpretation occurs.

One may object that there is a doubt as to the sense of sight being involved solely in reading.[8] For example, the sense of touch is engaged in reading braille. What about reading as an auditory experience when a text is read aloud in a communal setting, or phenomena such as the slight movement of vocal cords while reading? As to braille, I would think there is a distinction between deciphering written, linguistic symbols by touch and that of touching various textures, petting an animal, or placing one's hand in a running stream. While braille is an exception to the claim that reading is typically reduced to sight, what reading by sight and by touch, as in the case of braille, share in common is that each is interpreting linguistic symbols; whereas "carnal" interpretation of nonlinguistic entities is a mediation of the nonlinguistic by way of the flesh. Similarly, the auditory experience of hearing a text read aloud is not reading per se as it is receiving spoken linguistic symbols via the sense of hearing, which I would distinguish from the sense of hearing and interpreting, say, the crashing of waves or the sounds of wildlife. The central argument of this chapter is that interpretation is not reducible to text interpretation, and that when interpreting nonlinguistic entities, those entities cannot merely be reduced to a metaphorical text. So, while there are exceptions to the general claim that reading a text only engages the sense of sight, those exceptions are still involved in understanding linguistic symbols and remains distinct from how senses such as hearing or touch engage the nonlinguistic.

What of responses of the body in the act of reading such as silently or slightly moving one's lips and vocal cords? In this case, I am merely going through the motions of reading out loud without putting any volume to it. Interpretive activity is taking place via the sense of sight, but my moving lips and vocal cords are not in any sense interpreting. Or how about a response to reading where a text might "give me the chills" or some other such physical sensation? In these cases, the engagement or involvement of the body is a response or reaction to the act of reading. The physical sensations are not instances of the flesh as a medium of interpretation. Rather, these are responses to an interpretation of a text in the act of reading, perhaps kind of carnal intentionality. If a scene in a horror story I am reading causes the emotion of fright and it sends a chill up my spine, both the emotion and the physical response are intentionally about my reading of the passage.

In speaking, especially, of environmental hermeneutics, more of the body is engaged in taking in an environment. Even in the sense of sight, I am not seeing the environment as I see text on a page. I am visually taking in colors and textures, or perhaps the play of light within the branches and leaves of a tree. The only thing in common, as it pertains to sight, between a text and a forest is that they are both things that are seen. But the commonality ends there. Things that are seen are not reducible to one another by the fact of being seen, and many things are seen in very different ways depending on what kind of thing each happens to be. There are simply different things going on in reading a text and viewing a forest. Moreover, beyond the use of the sense of sight, other senses are engaged in interpreting an environment that are not so engaged in reading a text. Looking at nature as a book to be read does not take into account the way the sense of sight is engaged in nature (as opposed to how it is in a text) and ignores the other senses altogether. Understanding the meaning of words in a text vs. understanding an environment are not the same thing, although both are interpretation. This is why I say that interpreting environments cannot be reduced to the metaphor of the text. At best, the metaphor that could be considered besides that of the text is one of reading. And only if "reading" is used as a metaphor for understanding rather than its literal sense of reading a text. For what we understand of nature in interpretive activity encompasses far more in lived experience than what we do when we read.

How then does Ricoeur's text-centric hermeneutics inform environmental hermeneutics? If reading a text and experiencing an environment are two different things, how is a theory of hermeneutics based in the text of any value to environmental hermeneutics? To address these questions, I will first discuss a more general theory of interpretation. Then I will argue that Ricoeur's hermeneutics, although framed as a theory for interpreting texts, can be understood under this more general theory of interpretation.

A GENERAL HERMENEUTICS

Gadamer described hermeneutics as a word which refers to "many different levels of reflection," all of which he says are based on "the art of understanding, and art particularly required any time the meaning of something is not clear and unambiguous."[9] Richard E. Palmer argues that even to begin to understand what hermeneutics is as the interpretation of texts, it is important to understand "a general account of interpretation itself," that is, "what understanding and interpretation, as such, are."[10] For Palmer, to exist is to be constantly interpreting throughout each and every conscious moment of the day. This is not meant to imply that the individual is immediately conscious of interpreting. In our existence, the world presents itself to us. Being placed in the world means interpreting, making sense of the world around us. This is, in essence, prelinguistic. Even understanding literature, Palmer argues, "must be rooted in the more primal and encompassing modes of understanding that have to do with our very being-in-the world."[11]

In his efforts to "expand" hermeneutics to technoscience, Don Ihde argued that factors of the day, such as the overarching influence of science and technology, "calls for a new hermeneutics" that is focused on the more originary meaning of hermeneuein, what he calls, simply, "interpretive activity" or "thing interpretation." Ihde takes hermeneuein to not only to deal with language, "but also with perceptual phenomena (sensory interpretive activity)."[12] Ihde's work seems to anticipate the more recent developments of hermeneutics as "carnal," that is, the body as a medium of interpretation. Much like Palmer, Ihde seems to suggest that interpretation at root is more primal and prelinguistic.

Hermeneutics, it could be said, is the study of how we construe the world about us, how it is we come to an idea of what something means—that is, interpretation. Interpretation is typically not at play when meaning is immediate. For example, when I enter the freeway and see a speed limit sign, assuming I know the language in which the sign is written, I immediately know the fastest speed that I am permitted to drive. When I see an on/off switch on a device or appliance, and I want to either turn on or off the device or appliance, there is no ambiguity as to what I need to do. Another characteristic of these examples is that in addition to the meaning being apparent and grasped immediately, I need not discern between multiple potential meanings. Moreover, I do not need to adjudicate between conflicting meanings. The meaning is singular. A 35mph speed limit sign is open to only one understanding—do not exceed the limit designated on the sign. "Interpretation," writes Ricoeur, "is the work of thought which consists in deciphering the hidden meaning in apparent meaning, in unfolding levels of meaning implied in the literal meaning . . . there is interpretation wherever there is multiple meaning, and it is in interpretation that the plurality of meaning in made manifest."[13] Anything that can have hidden or multiple meanings requires interpretation. Texts require interpretation, but so do works of art and, of course, environments. And all things that we interpret are interpreted according to their own sets of rules and requirements, such as those I indicated above about which multiple senses are involved in the encounter with something and the apprehension of its meanings.

Life is a series of actions (what we do and practice) based on how we understand, judgments we make, and aspects of discernment in the course of lived experience. Hence, a general hermeneutics seems evident. This, of course, does not yet answer the question of how Ricoeur's text-centric hermeneutics can be drawn upon to develop an environmental hermeneutics. One may well recognize a general theory of interpretation, which would be necessary in environmental hermeneutics, and still argue that Ricoeur's hermeneutics of the text is too limited to apply to interpreting environments. In this next section, I will seek to overcome this objection.

TEXT AND MEANING

Ricoeur defines a text as "any discourse fixed by writing."[14] The text is distinguished from discourse in that, in discourse, the speaker and interlocutor have an immediate relation, whereas the text does not give the author (speaker) and reader (interlocutor) the immediate relation. In discourse, there is dialogue in which speaker and interlocutor may "exchange questions and answer" but "there is no exchange of this sort between the writer and the reader."[15] Communication is the nature of discourse, but such is not present between an author and a reader. This is why Ricoeur later goes on to say that interpretation becomes an "attitude"[16] one takes in relation to a text.

What is this attitude? To better understand this attitude toward the text, let us first go back to discourse. Ricoeur says that discourse is the realization of language, and that discourse is an event.[17] Language is "outside of time," being introduced into time in discourse; discourse is "realized temporally and in the present."[18] It is the temporal reality of discourse which makes it an event. This event, being temporal, is an instant in time. But it is not the instant of the "fleeting event" we wish to understand, but the "meaning that endures."[19] In discourse, being temporally bound in the instant, the meaning is found in the reference. The "reference" in terms of discourse is "the truth value of the proposition, its claim to reach reality."[20] In discourse, reference is concrete, temporal, and is directed to the real. The "sense" of the words of discourse (the language), being outside of time, "has no relation to reality, its words returning to other words in the endless circle of the dictionary."[21] But, in the saying of discourse, meanings are intended, Ricoeur says, and are directed to concrete reality.

What happens, though, to reference once the discourse is "fixed by writing" in the text? When the immediacy between speaker and interlocutor who share a "common reality" is erased by the text, in which a writer and reader do not share a common situation, what is the reference? What is the meaning? The comprehension of meaning in discourse is linked with the intention of the speaker, that is, the psychology of the speaker. However, the reader of a text does not have access to the "psychological intentions" of the writer to get to an intended meaning "behind the text."[22] This is what Ricoeur calls a "second-order reference" where interpretation is defined, not as getting to the psychology of the author but to "explicate that type of being-in-the-world unfolded in front of the text."[23] Ricoeur is distinguishing here interpretation as going behind to get to a psychological intention from interpretation as unfolding in front of. The meaning sought in this second-order reference of interpretation meaning that is contained in the text that is not bound to the finitude of the author's intention.

This is then what characterizes the attitude one takes when reading. Ricoeur says that reading moves the "text toward meaning,"[24] that is, a future-oriented movement. He further says that the text "calls for a reading" and that reading is only possible,

> because the text is not closed in on itself but opens out onto other things. To read is, on this hypothesis, to conjoin a new discourse to the discourse of the text. This conjunction of discourse reveals, in the very constitution of the text, an original capacity for renewal that is its open character. Interpretation is the concrete outcome of conjunction and renewal.[25]

Interpretation, in philosophical hermeneutics, is not a matter of discovering an originary meaning of a text found in the intention of the author. Rather, in recognizing the capacity of language to contain innumerable potential meanings beyond the author's intended meaning, hermeneutics understands that interpreting texts involves appropriating the text in one's own time and situation. Treating a text in this way does not mean that the reader can decide that a text can have any meaning the reader chooses. Ricoeur writes: "It is not a question of imposing upon the text our finite capacity for understanding, but exposing ourselves to the text and receiving from it an enlarged self, which would be the proposed existence corresponding in the most suitable way to the world proposed."[26] Gadamer noted that in interpretation there can be "a fluid multiplicity of possibilities" of meaning but "not everything is possible."[27] Again, the interpretation of a text is a forward-looking opening up to ways of being as we are exposed to the text and receive from it, to use Ricoeur's terminology. Can we now, based on Ricoeur's hermeneutics of the text, construct an environmental hermeneutics that does not rely on viewing environments as quasi-texts?

INTERPRETATIVE ACTIVITY

My claim here in answering the foregoing question is simply this: rather than assuming that hermeneutics first and foremost concerns the interpretation of texts that we then project as a metaphor onto other objects of interpretation, my assumption will be that hermeneutics is fundamentally about interpretive activity (Ihde) and a basic act of human thinking (Palmer) that is enacted anytime something is understood. What is understood can be a text, a work of art, an environment, a culture, any number of things. While there may be different variables or rules of interpretation for different kinds of things, such as how different things engage different senses, for instance, there is no need to assume the primacy of texts in hermeneutics that requires the metaphor of the text for interpretative activity generally. Therefore, Ricoeur's hermeneutics, even that which is primarily focused on texts, can provide rich insights and ways of understanding environments that do not require a "book of nature" approach.

One of the most important and relevant insights of Ricoeur's hermeneutics of the text that opens up pathways for environmental hermeneutics is the understanding of interpretation as an unfolding in front of rather than a discerning behind. One thing this essentially reveals is that interpretation is the result of an encounter, an exposure, as Ricoeur might say. Where a text is concerned, exposure happens in the act of reading. Where the environment is concerned, this exposure takes place in the flesh. Environmental hermeneutics and carnal hermeneutics, in this sense, are correlative. We do not "read" environments as we do texts, but whether a text or an environment, we are exposed, perhaps in different ways, but exposed, nonetheless. The whole point of this exposure is to receive from that to which we are exposed new ways of being in the world.

What is also at play here in this forward-looking aspect of interpretation is the autonomy of the text from the author. This has important implications for environmental hermeneutics. One objection or question I have encountered in conversation (most frequently at conferences) is that environments do not have authors as texts do, so how is it that we can speak of interpreting environments? In other words, texts have this characteristic of having been written by someone, but environments do not share this characteristic. There are several responses to this, which I will go over, but most of all is the fact that as far as hermeneutics is concerned, the author is incidental to the text and not relevant with regard to interpretation understood as unfolding *in-front-of*. Therefore, that an environment cannot be said to have an author is not relevant to understanding it. What I have just said, of course, sets aside the issue of religious belief that would refer to the book of nature whose author is its creator. Even so, the autonomy of the text from the author as fundamental to hermeneutics would equally apply to the notion of a creator. Even supposing a creator intended or inscribed particular meanings into nature, interpreting nature would not be a matter of the "psychology of the creator" but about meanings that open up *in-front-of* in the encounter.

Is this not the same in terms of most anything that is interpreted? Films have writers and producers, works of art are produced by artists, architectural structures have architects who design them, but whatever meaning that might be intended in the minds of these creators is eclipsed by the meanings that unfold from the autonomy of the work. There is no reason to look at films, art, or buildings as quasi-texts. The autonomy of the thing interpreted from its creator, whether writer or architect, is characteristic of interpretation (or interpretive activity) as such. Therefore, an author or creator is not a focus of interpretive activity, so if something lacks an author or creator, such as so-called natural environments, as an object of interpretation there is no difference. Finally, what is indisputable is that environments are, in fact, interpreted. It seems absurd to say "nature does not have an author like a text, so it cannot be interpreted." If environmental hermeneutics makes any contribution to the study of hermeneutics, it is that it reveals that a hermeneutics of texts is not the fundamental measure of hermeneutics itself.

ENVIRONMENTAL IDENTITY

Chapter 2 was devoted to the topic of environmental identity and its corporeality. Environmental identity also has something to contribute to the discussion of nature as text (and why nature need not be viewed as text-like). In Ricoeur's explanation of interpretation as being in front of and a way of explaining our "being-in-the-world" in front of the text, he goes on to illuminate how interpretation of a text also includes interpretation of self. We could say that understanding a text proposes new worlds, on the one hand, but must, therefore, include an understanding of how we are to be in that world. The question of how we are to be is a question of our sense of self—who we wish to be. How we orient ourselves in the world and act within it is revelatory of how we see ourselves. Ricoeur takes note (as he has in several works) that there is a pretension in the idea that the subject "knows itself by immediate intuition," when in fact "we understand ourselves only by the long detour of the signs of humanity deposited in cultural works."[28] This is why he says that the text is a medium of self-understanding.

Earlier, I spoke of how interpretation *in-front-of* was not imposing any meaning one chooses on a text. In this line of thought, Ricoeur writes: "So understanding is quite different from a constitution of which the subject would possess the key. In this respect, it would be more correct to say that the self is constituted by the 'matter' of the text" and that "the interpretation of a text culminates in the self-interpretation of a subject who thenceforth understands himself better, understands himself differently, or simply begins to understand himself."[29] This phenomenon of self-understanding through the transformative effect of reading, however, is not limited to reading—that is, the "text." Ricoeur writes elsewhere: "Every hermeneutics is thus, explicitly or implicitly, self-understanding by means of understanding others."[30]

As not to be misleading, in the passage just cited, Ricoeur is referring to the work of the exegete of historical texts, explaining how the exegete is to overcome historical distance and make familiar that which was alien and strange. The quote, then, does refer back to the text. But the historian, in interpreting the historical text, is seeking to overcome a cultural distance between himself or herself and that of people of an earlier time, the "world of the text" to which Ricoeur frequently referred in his work. Thus, Ricoeur does not say that every hermeneutics is self-understanding by understanding texts, but "by means of understanding others." As such, this is why I contend that Ricoeur's text-centric hermeneutics can be understood within a broader conception of hermeneutics such that his hermeneutic insights are useful for considering general hermeneutic experience and, therefore, environmental hermeneutics. In the spirit of Ricoeur's own explanation that meaning can unfold that an author did not intend, Ricoeur's words that "every hermeneutics" is a means of self-understanding by understanding others would seem to include environmental hermeneutics as well. To make the passage particular to environmental hermeneutics, the passage could be reworded to say: "Environmental hermeneutics entails self-understanding by means of understanding environmental others." This interpretation is further bolstered by Ricoeur's later work in Oneself as Another, representing his return to the body, where he stated that the "polysemic character of otherness . . . [is] not reduced to the otherness, as is too often taken for granted, to the otherness of another Person."[31]

Oneself as Another is surely a prime example of a post-text centric hermeneutics for Ricoeur in which he explicitly set out to develop a "hermeneutics of the self"—that is, interpretation of selfhood and identity. Further, Oneself as Another is absent any text metaphor reference wherein the self is likened to a text. In this work, the primary focus or "object" of interpretation is the self. In previous works, self-interpretation was considered as something that is entailed in the work of interpreting, but Oneself as Another goes into a greater analysis of selfhood itself. The notion of detours, of course, remains central, especially as it is expressed in the previously noted "third philosophical intention" where the self is constituted by passing through the other.

THE BOOK OF NATURE REVISITED

At this juncture, I would like to return to the notion of the book of nature and argue that, ironically, the book of nature can act as a medium through which objects of interpretation that are not texts can be freed from the metaphor of the text. Speaking of the extension of hermeneutics from biblical exegesis to a new hermeneutics not limited to "literary texts," Ricoeur writes:

> Still, the exegetical tradition affords a good starting point for our enterprise, for the notion of the text can be taken in an analogous sense. Thanks to the metaphor of "the book of nature" the Middle Ages was able to speak of an interpretatio naturae. This metaphor brings to light a possible extension of the notion of exegesis, inasmuch as the notion of the "text" is wider than that of "scripture."[32]

What is interesting here is that something that is not a text—i.e., nature—provided a way to not only expand hermeneutics from scriptural exegesis to other texts, but as Ricoeur goes on to say in this passage, the *interpretatio naturae* freed the "notion of the text" from the notions of scripture and writing itself! The metaphor of the text in nature freed the text from the text! Thus the scriptural model of exegesis is given up in favor of the *interpretatio naturae*. Ricoeur cites, among others, the example of Freud who employed the notion of the book of nature by describing an analyst's work as translation. Interpreting dreams is to look at the dream as "an unintelligible text for which the analyst substitutes a more intelligible text."[33] The book of nature opened up the possibility of bringing interpretation to any number of non-texts, but only by treating them as analogous to texts.

As I said above, the problem with the metaphor of the text is not that it is strictly wrong, but that it limits our concept of interpretation as such, especially for things other than texts that involve more of the body. An unexamined assumption appears to be that if the idea of interpretation began as scriptural exegesis (obviously bound to the text), then even the extension of the concept of interpretation beyond the text is still a form, if only analogously, of textual exegesis. The notion of the "book of nature" affords a means by which the analogy (or metaphor) of the text can be used in other non-textual objects of interpreting. But what if, rather than having to think in terms of the analogy, we simply realized that interpretation (the apprehension of meaning) is something that we are always doing as beings who "wonder" about things and who, as Aristotle said, have instilled in us the "desire to know" (Metaphysics, Book I, 980a21).

Interpretation considered as a fundamental human activity opens new and broader horizons for hermeneutics, as well as for a greater comprehension of the multiple means of how understanding takes place, for instance, via the medium of the flesh. Just as Ricoeur claimed that we can abandon the scriptural model in favor the interpretatio naturae for a new hermeneutics, perhaps now we can say that we can abandon the notion of the book of nature in favor of a more general theory of interpretation. We can recognize that the "book of nature" provided a way out of limiting hermeneutics to the scriptural exegetical model, but now recognize that the very notion of the interpretation of nature likewise eclipses the need for a metaphor of the text or a book of nature.

NATURE AND THE SPEAKABLE

Th environment can be interpreted without recourse to the notion of the book of nature, but that does not necessarily exclude a place for language in environmental hermeneutics. In fact, in light of the question of the relationship of human beings to other-than-human-nature, language is necessary to "save the environment" if that also means "saving ourselves." To cite this passage from the 1993 interview with Ricoeur once again: "Now, we know that for there to be humanity after us, there has to be nature after us; then, in this sense, the preservation of nature is a part of the humanist project."[34] As I argued in chapter 4, the question of the preservation of nature or saving the environment is one of human concern and only matters as long as we are here (as Ricoeur also said, as I covered in chapter 1, that as far as we know, we are the only beings who question). As language beings, then, language holds a central role in environmental hermeneutics and environmental discourse generally. Why? "It is first of all and always in language that all ontic or ontological understanding arrives at its expression."[35] According to Ricoeur, understanding takes place in language (expression), which follows hermeneutical reflection.

Ricoeur writes: "To say something of something is, in the complete and strong sense of the term, to interpret."[36] One way to define environmental hermeneutics, to adapt to Ricoeur's words here, is that to say something of the environment is to interpret the environment. It is here that I find another way to distinguish the idea of the book of nature (or nature as a text to be read) from what can be said and expressed about hermeneutical experience of environments. Keep in mind that, for Ricoeur, interpretation is aimed at the unfolding *in-front-of*, not to get behind to some originary meaning. This distinction is helpful and demonstrates that expressing lived experience of environments in language in no way regards environments as a text. Rather, the lived experience is the prelinguistic carnal experience, a saturated sensory experience, that is then articulated in front of the experience in language. One thing that is articulated as a result is an envisioned way of our shared being-in-the-world. A passage from Thoreau's *Walden* will serve to exemplify the argument. In the section titled "Solitude," Thoreau writes:

> This is a delicious evening, when the whole body is one sense, and imbibes delight through every pore. I go and come with a strange liberty in Nature, a part of herself. As I walk along the stony shore of the pond in my shirt sleeves, though it is cool as well as cloudy and windy, and I see nothing special to attract me, all the elements are unusually congenial to me. The bullfrogs trump to usher in the night, and the note of the whippoorwill is borne on the rippling wind from over the water. Sympathy with the fluttering alder and poplar leaves almost takes away my breath, yet, like the lake, my serenity is rippled but not ruffled.[37]

The linguistic imagery here is remarkable and an emblematic instance of carnal hermeneutics.[38] Consider the imagery. The evening is described as "delicious," a reference to the sense of taste, something to be savored. But, beyond any single sense or a distinction between all the senses, the "whole body is one sense, and imbibes delight through every pore." Nature is received, quite literally, through the medium of the flesh, each and every sense engaged. There is sympathy that leaves Thoreau's serenity, like the lake, only rippled, which he distinguishes from being ruffled. Being ruffled seems to indicate a kind of discordance or loss of peace, whereas a ripple speaks more of a response or interaction with the surroundings. Thoreau's description most assuredly requires proximity to with nature, but proximity is not to be conflated with immediacy.

Kearney makes this point in which he says that proximity, not being immediacy, preserves difference.[39] This resonates in Thoreau's description of his experience in that each aspect of the experience is defined by proximity (embodied relation with the surroundings), not by immediacy—Thoreau himself, the clouds and winds, the bullfrogs and whippoorwills, the lake itself, and so on, are never dissolved in one another, but the difference always preserved, which is what makes the experience meaningful. Immediacy would blur the lines. Yet, there is another important aspect to this distinction between proximity and immediacy. Immediacy would suggest a direct intuition characteristic of the cogito whereas proximity indicates a carnal nearness that is nonetheless mediated, which might be described in Ricoeurian terms as understanding that comes through detours. While many could be elaborated upon, one such detour is the lived experience in the flesh rather than a direct intuition in the mind in the Cartesian sense.

Here, though, is where I would like to point out what is apparent, so much so that it might be easily missed or simply overlooked. The proximate lived experience that Thoreau lived in the flesh is only known to us because it was expressed in language. Thoreau's experience is speakable (to use the Gadamerian term). If it were not speakable it would remain only in Thoreau's consciousness, unable to be communicated. It matters not that we only receive it in the modality of language in the text (rather than in actual discourse with a living Thoreau). The point is that it is in language that experience is expressed. Thoreau's embodied experience is articulated in language and, therefore, communicative. Environmental experience is speakable, to use Gadamer's term, indicating the experience itself is prelinguistic (in this case, carnal) but expressible in language. Without this expression in language, there would be no environmental discourse among human beings; and without environmental discourse, there is no way to imagine and initiate new worlds and new ways of being in the world that is necessary for "saving" the environment and, thereby, assuring a place for humanity after us.

Finally, another apparent fact is that not only is Thoreau's account mediated by language (the speakable), it is also specifically mediated via the mode of language of the text. Here I think back to Palmer where he notes that although interpretive experience can be and often is prelinguistic, it is nonetheless the case that "human existence as we know it does in fact always involve language."[40] Thus, while I am arguing for an understanding of hermeneutics that does not rely on the metaphor of the text, I do not deny that even environmental experience (or any nonlinguistic mode of interpretation) is mediated to others via the text. In Ricoeur's terms, we can say that the "event" of environmental experience is something about we can have discourse, and then, of course, that discourse can be "fixed" by writing. In the words of the magnificent and inspiring book *A Philosophy of Walking* by Frédéric Gros:

> Writing ought to be this: testimony to a wordless living experience. Not the commentary on another book, not the exegesis of another text. The book as witness . . . but witness in the sense of the baton in a relay race. Thus does the book, born out of experience, refer to that experience. Books are not to teach us how to live (that would be the sad task of lesson-givers), but to make us want to live, to live differently: to find in ourselves the possibility of life, its principle.[41]

Just above this passage, Gros says that Emerson had recalled that Thoreau was careful to not give more time to writing than he did to walking. For if one spent too much time in libraries, then what one writes would be "filled with the writing of others." The implication being that one's writing should be filled with the stuff of the wordless so that writing, in the spirit of Hermes, "brings a word from the realm of the wordless."[42] Is this not what Gadamer means when he states that being that can be understood is language? Furthermore, Gros's translator notes that the French word for "witness" in this passage, témoin, "has the subsidiary meaning of baton passed between runners in a relay race," hence the baton and relay race reference in the passage. Indeed, it is the case that the "wordless living experience," once translated into word, can mediate that experience to the reader, passing the baton of the experience we might say. But, to follow Thoreau's example, let us devote at least as much time to having the wordless living experiences themselves as we do to reading or writing about them.

CONCLUSION

We live in dire times. Hermeneutics is, of course, not the only discipline necessary to begin to answer the challenge of environmental problems such as climate change, issues of environmental justice, care and restoration of oceans, and so on. Still, hermeneutics has a great deal to offer. After all, environmental action is always an interpretation. What interpretations are and the conditions for interpretation need to be understood in the face of the environmental crisis. If hermeneutics, specifically environmental hermeneutics, is to aspire to its full potential, then it must escape the limitations of being understood as "the theory of the operations of understanding in their relation to the interpretation of texts" (see note 2). Hermeneutics must become more "carnal" if we are to speak of the earth and our relationship to it. For, indeed, our relationship to the earth is primarily an embodied one, not one of the Cartesian mind. Although I would use the terminology of "polycentrism" over "biocentrism" or "cosmocentrism," these words from Sallie McFague capture the necessity of what I would call the carnality of environmental hermeneutics:

> If the ecological crisis is calling for an end to a narrow anthropocentrism as our moral code (what is good for us and especially "me and my tribe"), then embodiment may move us not only toward a more biocentric and cosmocentric perspective but also toward a more inclusive sense of justice for the needs of all (embodied) human beings.[43]

Much of this chapter has been aimed at demonstrating that the metaphor of the text or the notion of the book of nature is not adequate to address the crisis we face. A focus on the body is necessary. Brian Treanor argues that since we pretty much do everything in the body or as a body, "it seems worthwhile to reflect on the nature of our embodiment, to understand what it is like and how it shapes our capabilities, powers, and limitations, and to appreciate the ways in which it determines our engagement with ourselves, with others, and with the world."[44] In the footnote to this citation, Treanor suggests that bringing together a "carnal hermeneutics of the body and an earthy hermeneutics of place" would make "substantial contributions" in addition to other hermeneutic accounts of things and how we ought to live, such as text-focused accounts.

What I have specifically argued for in this chapter is that the metaphor of the text or the notion of the book of nature limits the way environments and nature can be interpreted. As such, a more general hermeneutics that considers the many things we interpret and the many ways we interpret them (especially with and in the body) is needed. Despite its text-centricity, Ricoeur's hermeneutics can be adapted such that it can be employed in the service of an "earthy" hermeneutics and address modern day environmental problems. Ricoeur's hermeneutics of interpreting texts seems to contain within it insights and tools that beg to go beyond the text and unfold in front of the text to address itself to both our bodies and the earth.

NOTES

1. I briefly mentioned the problem of the metaphor of the text near the end of chapter 2 and, in a note, also mentioned my colleague Prof. Brian Treanor, with whom I've shared discussions off and on over the years on this topic. Treanor will have an essay titled "Earthy Hermeneutics: Beyond the Metaphor of the Text," in a forthcoming collection of essays devoted to environmental hermeneutics.

2. Paul Ricoeur, *From Text to Action: Essays in Hermeneutics, II*, translated by Kathleen Blamey and John B. Thompson (Evanston, IL: Northwestern University Press 1991), 53.

3. For an overview of the history of the concept of the "Book of Nature," I refer the reader to an essay by Forrest Clingerman titled, "Reading the Book of Nature: A Hermeneutical Account of Nature for Philosophical Theology," in *Worldviews* 13 (2009), 72–91.

4. Hans-Georg Gadamer, *Truth and Method*, Second revised edition, translation revised by Joel Weinsheimer and Donald G. Marshall (New York: Continuum, 1989 [2004]), 470.

5. Hans-Georg Gadamer, *Philosophical Hermeneutics*, translated and edited by David E. Linge (Berkeley: University of California Press, 1976), 67.

6. Ricoeur, *From Text to Action*, 106.

7. See Richard Kearney and Brian Treanor, editors, *Carnal Hermeneutics* (New York: Fordham University Press, 2015).

8. I am grateful to one of the anonymous reviewers for bringing these exceptions to the rule to my attention.

9. Hans-Georg Gadamer, *The Gadamer Reader: A Bouquet of Later Writings*, edited by Richard E. Palmer (Evanston, IL: Northwestern University Press, 2007), 44.

10. Richard E. Palmer, *Hermeneutics: Interpretation Theory in Schleiermacher, Dilthey, Heidegger, and Gadamer* (Evanston, IL: Northwestern University Press, 1969), 8.

11. Palmer, *Hermeneutics*, 10.

12. Don Ihde, *Expanding Hermeneutics: Visualism in Science* (Evanston, IL: North-western University Press, 1998), 2, 7–8.

13. Paul Ricoeur, *The Conflict of Interpretations: Essays in Hermeneutics* (Evanston, IL: Northwestern University Press, 1974), 13. Emphasis original.

14. Ricoeur, *From Text to Action*, 106.

15. Ricoeur, *From Text to Action*, 107.

16. Ricoeur, *From Text to Action*, 118.

17. See the chapter "The Hermeneutical Function of Distanciation" in *From Text to Action*.

18. Ricoeur, *From Text to Action*, 77.

19. Ricoeur, *From Text to Action*, 78.

20. Ricoeur, *From Text to Action*, 85.

21. Ricoeur, *From Text to Action*, 85.

22. Ricoeur, *From Text to Action*, 85–86. Emphasis original.

23. Ricoeur, *From Text to Action*, 86. Emphasis original.

24. Ricoeur, *From Text to Action*, 118.

25. Ricoeur, *From Text to Action*, 118.

26. Ricoeur, *From Text to Action*, 88.

27. Hans-Georg Gadamer, *Truth and Method*, 271.

28. Ricoeur, *From Text to Action*, 87.

29. Ricoeur, *From Text to Action*, 88, 118.

30. Ricoeur, *The Conflict of Interpretations*, 17. Emphasis mine.

31. Paul Ricoeur, *Oneself as Another*, translated by Kathleen Blamey (Chicago: University of Chicago Press, 1992), 317.

32. Paul Ricoeur, *Freud and Philosophy: An Essay on Interpretation*, translated by Denis Savage (New Haven: Yale University Press, 1970), 24–25.

33. Ricoeur, *Freud and Philosophy*, 25.

34. Paul Ricoeur, *Philosophy, Ethics, & Politics*, edited by Catherine Goldenstein and translated by Kathleen Blamey (Cambridge, UK: Polity Press, 2020), 114.

35. Ricoeur, *The Conflict of Interpretations*, 11.

36. Ricoeur, *Freud and Philosophy*, 22.

37. Henry David Thoreau, *Walden; or, Life in the Woods* (New York: Barnes & Noble Classics, 2005), 104. The original publication year of *Walden* was 1854.

38. This section of the chapter is exemplary of the arguments presented by Richard Kearney in, "The Wager of Carnal Hermeneutics," in Kearney and Treanor, editors, *Carnal Hermeneutics*, 15–56. I think, especially, of the early part of Kearney's essay where he discusses the notion of "evaluation" in embodied life, signified by *sapientia*,

meaning "wisdom," that is related to the idea of savoring (16); and his analysis of Aristotle on the flesh as a medium (not merely an organ) of interpretation (18).

39. Kearney, "The Wager of Carnal Hermeneutics," 19.

40. Palmer, *Hermeneutics*, 9.

41. Frédéric Gros, *A Philosophy of Walking*, translated by John Howe (London: Verso, 2015), 95. Emphasis original.

42. Don Ihde, *Expanding Hermeneutics: Visualism in Science* (Evanston, IL: Northwestern University Press, 1998), 9. Emphasis original.

43. Sallie McFague, *The Body of God: An Ecological Theology* (Minneapolis: Fortress Press, 1993), 48.

44. Brian Treanor, "Mind the Gap: The Challenge of Matter," in *Carnal Hermeneutics*, 58.

Conclusion

This book is far more abstract (more than I would have liked, even though I wrote it) than it is practical. Yet, all practice is rooted in conviction and ideas. What is done now and in the coming years with regard to the planet will be preceded by thought, especially thought as interpretation. Although the great majority of this book is more theory than practice, I believe that it provides groundwork for environmental practice. I concur with J. Baird Callicott: "Environmental Philosophy *Is* Environmental Activism: The Most Radical and Effective Kind."[1] Callicott, in this chapter of that title, distinguishes two representations of philosophy, the first being the stereotype of ivory tower where academics, closed off from the "real world" contemplating questions of no practical worth, and the second calls Socrates to mind. Socrates was tried and ultimately put to death. Why? Did he commit some heinous crime? His crime was questioning the status quo and, thereby, stirring the city of Athens to improve.

While there is plenty of socially and politically irrelevant philosophy (which is not to say that it is bad or is not good for its own sake), the heart of philosophy is to matter to our lives and our shared world. It is in this spirit that I have written this book. As Callicott says: "In thinking, talking, and writing about environmental ethics, environmental philosophers already have their shoulders to the wheel, helping to reconfigure the prevailing cultural worldview and thus helping to push general practice in the direction of environmental responsibility."[2] Of course, to be effective and successful, environmental philosophers (and environmental hermeneuticists!), we philosophers are going to have to talk with those other than fellow philosophers. But the point is that theory is not anti-practical. In fact, I would argue that there is no practice without theory. There is no action without ideas. The aim is to be self-conscious of our theories and ideas so that we may act with greater confidence and conviction.

Philosophical hermeneutics is about the interpretive character of human life. We do not have to intend to interpret, it is simply what we do, and our conduct is driven by interpretation. Gadamer wrote: "I maintain that the hermeneutical problem is universal and the basis for all interhuman experience, both of history and of the present moment, precisely because meaning can be experienced even where it is not actually intended."[3] Gadamer went on to object to those who think that hermeneutics lies outside the world of the concrete and "real" factors of the world. Where, precisely, does interpretation take place? It happens in the world and is about the world. It seems to me that our relationship to the planet and our environment is the place *par excellence* where hermeneutics belongs.

Paul Ricoeur, especially, was so engaged with so many and varied dialogue partners and disciplines, that I think his work is uniquely potential-laden to address environmental problems. Even if Ricoeur never did any systematic philosophical work on environmental issues, his work (as I have tried to show in this book) presents ways of thinking about the world that address our fundamental way of being in the world and, therefore, is a tremendous resource for environmental hermeneutics. But there is still even further work to be done from the thought of Paul Ricoeur. In this book, I said little about the critique of ideology, for example. It would not be far off (if at all) to say that our environmental crisis is a crisis of ideology and the critique that is inherent to hermeneutics is needed to confront ideologies of environmental destruction.

The environmental crisis is also a political crisis, in the sense of the *polis*. Environmental hermeneutics, in this sense, must also be political. Donatella Di Cesare has recently published a powerful book, *The Political Vocation of Philosophy*,[4] that calls for philosophy to return to the *polis* and defends relevance of philosophy for politics. What she writes of philosophy generally, I would hold to be true for hermeneutics especially. Lorenzo C. Simpson has recently published an excellent work recognizing this fact titled *Hermeneutics as Critique*.[5] The scope of the environmental crisis calls for a hermeneutics that is radical and political. The universality of hermeneutics has never been so clear, in my view, than it is today.

Back to the idea of theory and practice, Ricoeur firmly believed that theory (saying) and practice (doing) are inseparable, the latter being predicated on the former. While some would argue that theory is useless and we need to act because of the dire situation we are in environmentally, Ricoeur (speaking in the context of work) asks "what would the civilization of work be without the splendor and vanity of the word?"[6] For Ricoeur, the word and work, or theory and practice, are counterparts. He was also aware that the word could also produce, not a civilization of splendor, but also one of injustice. This is why we must be ever so mindful that our words, where interpretation dwells, are creative and point to the kind of world in which we wish to live.

If hermeneutics can be described as saying something to someone about something, I would add what also can be said of hermeneutics is that it is aimed at doing something with someone about something. As Ricoeur said, "living with and for others in just institutions." A Ricoeurian environmental hermeneutics and environmental hermeneutics generally should be saying something to many about the environmental crisis so that we can collectively do something about it. Ricoeur observed that we are but a "fragment" of the ecosystem. Humanity seems to have forgotten this truth. For the planet and humanity to be whole, we need to learn once more what it means to be just a fragment.

NOTES

1. This is the title of the second chapter of Callicott's book *Beyond the Land Ethic: More Essays in Environmental Philosophy* (Albany: SUNY Press, 1999), 27–43.

2. Callicott, *Beyond the Land Ethic*, 43.

3. Hans-Georg Gadamer, *Philosophical Hermeneutics*, translated and edited by David E. Linge (Berkeley: University of California Press, 1976), 30.

4. Donatella Di Cesare, *The Political Vocation of Philosophy*, translated by David Broder (Cambridge, UK: Polity Press, 2021).

5. Lorenzo C. Simpson, *Hermeneutics as Critique: Science, Politics, Race, and Culture* (New York: Columbia University Press, 2021).

6. Paul Ricoeur, *History and Truth*, translated with an introduction by Charles A. Kelbley (Evanston, IL: Northwestern University Press, 1965), 210.

Bibliography

Angus, Ian. *Facing the Anthropocene: Fossil Capitalism and the Crisis of the Earth System*. Foreword by John Bellamy Foster. New York: Monthly Review Press, 2016.

Arendt, Hannah "Understanding and Politics (The Difficulties of Understanding)" in *Essays in Understanding, 1930–1954: Formation, Exile, and Totalitarianism*. Edited and with an introduction by Jerome Kohn. New York: Schocken Books, 1994, 307–27.

Beckerman, Wilfred, and Joanna Pasek. "In Defense of Anthropocentrism." In *Environmental Ethics: The Big Questions*. Chichester, UK: Wiley-Blackwell, 2010, 83–88.

Bell, Nathan. "Environmental Hermeneutics with and for Others: Ricoeur's Ethics and the Ecological Self." In *Interpreting Nature: The Emerging Field of Environmental Hermeneutics*, edited by Forrest Clingerman, Brian Treanor, Martin Drenthen, and David Utsler. New York: Fordham University Press, 2014, 141–59.

Benjamin, Walter. *Illuminations: Essays and Reflections*. Translated by Harry Zohn. Edited and with an introduction by Hannah Arendt. New York: Schocken Books, 1968.

Brown, Charles S. "Anthropocentrism and Ecocentrism: The Quest for a New Worldview." In *The Midwest Quarterly* 36, no. 2 (1995): 191–202.

Callicott, J. Baird. *Beyond the Land Ethic: More Essays in Environmental Philosophy*. Albany: SUNY Press, 1999.

Cameron, W.S.K. "Must Environmental Philosophy Relinquish the Concept of Nature? A Hermeneutic Reply to Steven Vogel." In *Interpreting Nature: The Emerging Field of Environmental Hermeneutics*, edited by Forrest Clingerman, Brian Treanor, Martin Drenthen, and David Utsler, 102–20. New York: Fordham University Press, 2014.

Carson, Rachel. *Silent Spring*, 50th Anniversary Edition. Boston: Mariner Books, 2002.

Cesare, Donatella Ester Di. *Utopia of Understanding: Between Babel and Auschwitz*. Translated by Niall Keane. Albany: SUNY Press, 2012.

Cesare, Donatella Di. *The Political Vocation of Philosophy*. Translated by David Broder. Cambridge, UK: Polity Press, 2021.

Clayton, Susan, and Susan Opotow, editors. *Identity and the Natural Environment: The Psychological Significance of Nature*. Cambridge, MA: The MIT Press, 2003.

Clingerman, Forrest. "Reading the Book of Nature: A Hermeneutical Account of Nature for Philosophical Theology." In *Worldviews* 13 (2009): 72–91.

Clingerman, Forrest, Brian Treanor, Martin Drenthen, and David Utsler, editors. *Interpreting Nature: The Emerging Field of Environmental Hermeneutics*. New York: Fordham University Press, 2014.

Crutzen, Paul J., and Eugene F. Stoermer. "The Anthropocene." *Global Change Newsletter* 41 (2000): 17–18.

Descola, Philippe. *Beyond Nature and Culture*. Translated by Janet Lloyd. Chicago: University of Chicago Press, 2013.

Empson, Martin, editor. *System Change Not Climate Change*. London: Bookmarks Publications, 2019.

Feenberg, Andrew. *The Ruthless Critique of Everything Existing: Nature and Revolution in Marcuse's Philosophy of Praxis*. Brooklyn: Verso Books, 2023.

Figueroa, Robert Melchior. "Evaluating Environmental Justice Claims." In *Forging Environmentalism: Justice, Livelihood and Contested Environments*. Edited by Joanne Bauer. New York: M.E. Sharpe, 2006.

Fisher, Mark. *Capitalist Realism: Is There No Alternative?* Washington: Zero Books, 2009.

Foster, John Bellamy. *Capitalism in the Anthropocene: Ecological Ruin or Ecological Revolution*. New York: Monthly Review Press, 2022.

Gadamer, Hans-Georg. *Philosophical Hermeneutics*. Translated and edited by David E. Linge. Berkeley: University of California Press, 1976.

Gadamer, Hans-Georg. *Truth and Method*. Second, Revised Edition, translation revised by Joel Weinsheimer and Donald G. Marshall. New York: Continuum, 2004 [1989].

Gadamer, Hans-Georg. *The Gadamer Reader: A Bouquet of Later Writings*. Edited by Richard E. Palmer. Evanston, IL: Northwestern University Press, 2007.

George, Theodore. *The Responsibility to Understand: Hermeneutical Contours of the Ethical Life*. Edinburgh: Edinburgh University Press, 2020.

Gros, Frédéric. *A Philosophy of Walking*. Translated by John Howe. London: Verso, 2015.

Hanscom, Angela J. *Balanced and Barefoot: How Unrestricted Outdoor Play Makes for Strong, Confident, and Capable Children*. Oakland: New Harbinger Publications, Inc., 2016.

Haraway, Donna. *The Companion Species Manifesto: Dogs, People, and Significant Otherness*. Chicago: Prickly Paradigm Press, 2003.

Hargrove, Eugene C. *Foundations of Environmental Ethics*. Denton: Environmental Ethics Books, 1989.

Hayward, Tim "Anthropocentrism: A Misunderstood Problem." *Environmental Values* 6, no. 1 (1997): 49–63.

Heidegger, Martin. "Letter on Humanism." In *Basic Writings*. New York: Harper Perennial Modern Thought, 2008.

Heidegger, Martin. *Being and Time*. Translated by Joan Stambaugh with revisions by Dennis J. Schmidt. Albany: SUNY Press, 2010.

Helenius, Timo. "Culture as the Necessary Extension of Bodily Being." In *Paul Ricoeur and the Lived Body*. Edited by Roger W.H. Savage, 127–51. Lanham, MD: Lexington Books, 2020.

Horton, Sarah, Stephen Mendelsohn, Christine Rojcewicz, and Richard Kearney, editors. *Somatic Desire: Recovering Corporeality in Contemporary Thought*. Lanham, MD: Lexington Books, 2019.

Huber, Matthew T. *Climate Change as Class War: Building Socialism on a Warming Planet*. London: Verso, 2022.

Hull, R. Bruce. *Infinite Nature*.Chicago: University of Chicago Press, 2006.

Ihde, Don. *Expanding Hermeneutics: Visualism in Science*. Evanston, IL: Northwestern University Press, 1998.

Ihde, Don. *Postphenomenology and Technoscience: The Peking Lectures*. Albany: SUNY Press, 2009.

The International Panel on Climate Change, *Climate Change 2022: Impacts, Adaptation and Vulnerability* (2022).

Jonas, Hans. *The Imperative of Responsibility: In Search of an Ethics for the Technological Age*. Translated by Hans Jonas with the Collaboration of David Herr. Chicago: University of Chicago Press, 1984.

Kearney, Richard. *On Stories*. New York: Routledge, 2002.

Kearney, Richard, "Introduction: Ricoeur's Philosophy of Translation." In Paul Ricoeur, *On Translation*, translated by Eileen Brennan (New York: Routledge, 2006).

Kearney, Richard. "The Wager of Carnal Hermeneutics." In Richard Kearney and Brian Treanor, editors. *Carnal Hermeneutics*. New York: Fordham University Press, 2015.

Kearney, Richard. "Between Flesh and Text: Ricoeur's Carnal Hermeneutics." *Eco-ethica* 5 (2016): 219–31.

Kearney, Richard. *Touch: Recovering Our Most Vital Sense*. New York: Columbia University Press, 2021.

Kearney, Richard, and Brian Treanor, editors. *Carnal Hermeneutics*. New York: Fordham University Press, 2015.

Kearney, Richard, and Melissa Fitzpatrick. *Radical Hospitality: From Thought to Action* (New York: Fordham University Press), 2021.

Keller David R., editor. *Environmental Ethics: The Big Questions*. Chichester, UK: Wiley-Blackwell, 2010.

Klein, Naomi. *This Changes Everything: Capitalism vs. the Climate*. New York: Simon & Schuster, 2014

Louv, Richard. *Last Child in the Woods*. Chapel Hill, NC: Algonquin Books of Chapel Hill, 2008.

Louv, Richard. *The Nature Principle: Reconnecting with Life in a Virtual Age*. Chapel Hill, NC: Algonquin Books of Chapel Hill, 2012.

Malm, Andreas. *Fossil Capital: The Rise of Steam Power and the Roots of Global Warming*. London: Verso, 2016.

McFague, Sallie. *The Body of God: An Ecological Theology*. Minneapolis: Fortress Press, 1993.

Midgley, Mary. "The End of Anthropocentrism." In *Environmental Ethics: The Big Questions*. Chichester, UK: Wiley-Blackwell, 2010, 137–42.

Moore, Jason W., editor. *Anthropocene or Capitalocene: Nature, History, and the Crisis of Capitalism*. Oakland: PM Press, 2016.

Nietzsche, Friedrich Wilhelm. *The Gay Science: Or, the Joyful Wisdom*. Whithorn: Anodos Books, 2019.

Norton, Bryan G. "Environmental Ethics and Weak Anthropocentrism." *Environmental Ethics* 6, no. 2 (1984): 131–48.

Palmer, Richard. *Hermeneutics: Interpretation Theory in Schleiermacher, Dilthey, Heidegger, and Gadamer*. Evanston, IL: Northwestern University Press, 1969.

Peterson, Keith R. *A World Not Made for Us: Topics in Critical Environmental Philosophy*. Albany: SUNY Press, 2020.

Plumwood, Val. *Feminism and the Mastery of Nature*. London: Routledge, 1993.

Plumwood, Val. *Environmental Culture: The ecological crisis of reason*. London: Routledge, 2002.

Reagan, Charles E. *Paul Ricoeur: His Life and Work*. Chicago: University of Chicago Press, 1996.

Ricoeur, Paul. *History and Truth*. Translated with an introduction by Charles A. Kelbley. Evanston, IL: Northwestern University Press, 1965.

Ricoeur, Paul. *Freedom and Nature: The Voluntary and the Involuntary*. Translated by Erazim V. Kohák. Evanston, IL: Northwestern University Press, 1966.

Ricoeur, Paul. *Freud and Philosophy: An Essay on Interpretation*. Translated by Denis Savage. New Haven: Yale University Press, 1970.

Ricoeur, Paul. *The Conflict of Interpretations*. Edited by Don Ihde. Evanston, IL: Northwestern University Press, 1974.

Ricouer, Paul. *Hermeneutics and the Human Sciences: Essays on Language, Action, and Interpretation*. Edited and translated by John B. Thompson. Cambridge, UK: Cambridge University Press, 1981.

Ricoeur, Paul. *Time and Narrative. Vol. I*. Translated by Kathleen Blamey and David Pellauer. Chicago: University of Chicago Press, 1984.

Ricoeur, Paul. *Time and Narrative, Vol. 3*. Translated by Kathleen Blamey and David Pellauer. Chicago: University of Chicago Press, 1988.

Ricoeur, Paul. *From Text to Action: Essays in Interpretation, II*. Translated by Kathleen Blamey and John B. Thompson. Evanston, IL: Northwestern University Press, 1991.

Ricoeur, Paul. *Oneself as Another*. Translated by Kathleen Blamey. Chicago: University of Chicago Press, 1992.

Ricoeur, Paul. *The Course of Recognition*. Translated by David Pellauer. Cambridge, MA: Harvard University Press, 2005.

Ricoeur, Paul. *On Translation*. Translated by Eileen Brennan with an Introduction by Richard Kearney. New York: Routledge, 2006.

Ricoeur Paul. *Philosophy, Ethics, & Politics*. Edited by Catherine Goldenstein. Translated by Kathleen Blamey. Cambridge, UK: Polity Press, 2020.

Ricoeur, Paul. *Politics, Economy, and Society: Writings and Lectures, Volume 4*. Translated by Kathleen Blamey. Cambridge, UK: Polity Press, 2021.

Risser, James. *The Life of Understanding: A Contemporary Hermeneutics.* Bloomington: Indiana University Press, 2012.

Samuelsson, Lars. "At the Centre of What?" *Environmental Values* 22, no. 25 (October 2013): 627–45.

Secretariat of the Convention on Biological Diversity. "Message from Mr. Ahmed Djoghlaf, Executive Secretary, on the Occasion of the International Day for Biological Diversity, 22 May 2007." Accessed April 14, 2023. https://www.cbd.int /doc/speech/2007/sp-2007-05-22-es-en.pdf.

Simpson, Lorenzo C. *Hermeneutics as Critique: Science, Politics, Race, and Culture.* New York: Columbia University Press, 2021.

Sturgeon, Noël. *Ecofeminist Natures: Race, Gender, Feminist Theory and Political Action.* New York: Routledge, 1997.

Thoreau, Henry David. *Walden; or, Life in the Woods.* New York: Barnes & Noble Classics, 2005.

Treanor, Brian. *Emplotting Virtue: A Narrative Approach to Environmental Virtue Ethics.* Albany: SUNY Press, 2014.

Treanor, Brian. "Mind the Gap: The Challenge of Matter." In Richard Kearney and Brian Treanor, editors. *Carnal Hermeneutics.* New York: Fordham University Press, 2015.

Treanor, Brian, and James L. Taylor, editors. *Anacarnation and Returning to the Lived Body with Richard Kearney.* New York: Routledge, 2023.

Utsler, David. "Paul Ricoeur's Hermeneutics as a Model for Environmental Philosophy." *Philosophy Today* 53, no. 2 (Summer 2009): 173–78.

Utsler, David. "Who am I, Who Ae These People, and What Is the Place? A Hermeneutic Account of Self, Others, and Environments." In *Placing Nature on the Borders of Religion, Philosophy and Ethics*, edited by Forrest Clingerman and Mark Dixon, 139–51. Burlington: Ashgate Publishing, 2011.

Utsler, David. "Environmental Hermeneutics and Environmental/Eco-Psychology: Explorations in Environmental Identity." In *Interpreting Nature: The Emerging Field of Environmental Hermeneutics*, edited by Forrest Clingerman, Brian Treanor, Martin Drenthen, and David Utsler, 123–40. New York: Fordham University Press, 2014.

Utsler, David. "Is Nature Natural? And Other Linguistic Conundrums: Scott Cameron's Hermeneutic Defense of the Concept of Nature." *Environmental Philosophy* 15, no. 1 (Spring 2018): 77–89.

Utsler, David, and Cynthia Nielsen. "(Environmental) Hermeneutics at the Heart of the Anthropocene: Ricoeurian and Gadamerian Perspectives." In *Analecta Hermeneutica* 13 (2021): 52–72.

Vogel, Steven. *Against Nature: The Concept of Nature in Critical Theory.* Albany: SUNY Press, 1996.

Vogel, Steven. *Thinking Like a Mall: Environmental Philosophy After the End of Nature.* Cambridge, MA: MIT Press, 2016.

Warren, Karen J. *Ecofeminist Philosophy: A Western Perspective on What It Is and Why It Matters.* Lanham: Rowman & Littlefield, 2000.

Weston, Anthony. "Multicentrism: A Manifesto." *Environmental Ethics* 26, no. 1 (2004): 25–40.

Weston, Anthony. *The Incompleat Eco-Philosopher: Essays from the Edges of Environmental Ethics*. Albany: SUNY Press, 2009.

White, John R. "Lived Body and Ecological Value Cognition." In *Merleau-Ponty and Environmental Philosophy: Dwelling on the Landscapes of Thought*, edited by Suzanne L. Cataldi and William S. Hamrick, 177–89. Albany: SUNY Press, 2007.

Wood, David. *Reoccupy Earth: Notes toward an Other Beginning*. New York: Fordham University Press, 2019.

Index

About the Author

David Utsler teaches philosophy at North Central Texas College. He is coeditor of *Interpreting Nature: The Emerging Field of Environmental Hermeneutics* and has published peer-reviewed articles in journals such as *Philosophy Today*, *Environmental Philosophy*, and *Analecta Hermeneutica*. David is the codirector of the International Association for Environmental Philosophy and serves on the International Research Team for the project Hermeneutics of Architecture: Dwelling in the Horizon of Finitude, cosponsored by the International Institute for Hermeneutics, the University of Coimbra, and the University of Warsaw.

Milton Keynes UK
Ingram Content Group UK Ltd.
UKHW041630060924
447987UK00004B/65

9 781666 924893